THE BOY WHO LOST HIS FACE

LOUIS SACHAR

WORKBOOK

The Boy Who Lost His Face (얼굴을 잃어버린 소년)

1판 1쇄　2014년　1월 2일
2판 3쇄　2024년　4월 1일

지은이　Louis Sachar
기획　김승규
책임편집　김보경 정소이
콘텐츠제작및감수　롱테일 교육 연구소
저작권　명채린
디자인　김진영
마케팅　두잉글 사업 본부

펴낸이　이수영
펴낸곳　롱테일북스
출판등록　제2015-000191호
주소　04033 서울특별시 마포구 양화로 113, 3층(서교동, 순흥빌딩)
전자메일　help@ltinc.net

ISBN 979-11-91343-88-5　14740

Contents

'아동 도서계의 노벨상!' 미국 최고 권위의 아동 문학상

뉴베리 상(Newbery Award)은 미국 도서관 협회에서 해마다 미국 아동 문학 발전에 가장 크게 이바지한 작가에게 수여하는 아동 문학상입니다. 1922년에 시작된 이 상은 미국에서 가장 오랜 역사를 지닌 아동 문학상이자, '아동 도서계의 노벨상'이라 불릴 만큼 높은 권위를 자랑하는 상입니다.

뉴베리 상은 그 역사와 권위만큼이나 심사 기준이 까다롭기로 유명한데, 심사단은 책의 주제 의식은 물론 정보의 깊이와 스토리의 정교함, 캐릭터와 문체의 적정성 등을 꼼꼼히 평가하여 수상작을 결정합니다.

그해 최고의 작품으로 선정된 도서에게는 '뉴베리 메달(Newbery Medal)'이라고 부르는 금색 메달을 수여하며, 최종 후보에 올랐던 주목할 만한 작품들에게는 '뉴베리 아너(Newbery Honor)'라는 이름의 은색 마크를 수여합니다.

뉴베리 상을 받은 도서는 미국의 모든 도서관에 비치되어 더 많은 독자들을 만나게 되며, 대부분 수십에서 수백만 부가 판매되는 베스트셀러가 됩니다. 뉴베리 상을 수상한 작가는 그만큼 필력과 작품성을 인정받게 되어, 수상 작가의 다른 작품들 또한 수상작 못지않게 커다란 주목과 사랑을 받습니다.

왜 뉴베리 수상작인가?
쉬운 어휘로 쓰인 '검증된' 영어원서!

뉴베리 수상작들은 '검증된 원서'로 국내 영어 학습자들에게 큰 사랑을 받고 있습니다. 뉴베리 수상작이 원서 읽기에 좋은 교재인 이유는 무엇일까요?

1. 아동 문학인 만큼 어휘가 어렵지 않습니다.
2. 어렵지 않은 어휘를 사용하면서도 '문학상'을 수상한 만큼 문장의 깊이가 상당합니다.
3. 적당한 난이도의 어휘와 깊이 있는 문장으로 구성되어 있기 때문에 초등 고학년부터 성인까지, 영어 초보자부터 실력자까지 모든 영어 학습자들이 읽기에 좋습니다.

실제로 뉴베리 수상작은 국제중·특목고에서는 입시 필독서로, 대학교에서는 영어 강독 교재로 다양하고 폭넓게 활용되고 있습니다. 이런 이유로 뉴베리 수상작은 한국어 번역서보다 오히려 원서가 훨씬 많이 판매되는 기현상을 보이고 있습니다.

'베스트 오브 베스트'만을 엄선한 「뉴베리 컬렉션」

「뉴베리 컬렉션」은 뉴베리 메달 및 아너 수상작, 그리고 뉴베리 수상 작가의 유명 작품들을 엄선하여 한국 영어 학습자들을 위한 최적의 교재로 재탄생시킨 영어 원서 시리즈입니다.

1. 어휘 수준과 문장의 난이도, 분량 등 국내 영어 학습자들에게 적합한 정도를 종합적으로 검토하여 선정하였습니다.
2. 기존 원서 독자층 사이의 인기도까지 감안하여 최적의 작품들을 선별하였습니다.
3. 판형이 좁고 글씨가 작아 읽기 힘들었던 원서 디자인을 대폭 수정하여, 판형을 시원하게 키우고 읽기에 최적화된 영문 서체를 사용하여 가독성을 극대화하였습니다.
4. 함께 제공되는 워크북은 어려운 어휘를 완벽하게 정리하고 이해력을 점검하는 퀴즈를 덧붙여 독자들이 원서를 보다 쉽고 재미있게 읽을 수 있도록 구성하였습니다.
5. 기존에 높은 가격에 판매되어 구입이 부담스러웠던 오디오북을 부록으로 제공하여 리스닝과 소리 내어 읽기에까지 원서를 두루 활용할 수 있도록 했습니다.

루이스 새커(Louis Sachar)는 현재 미국에서 가장 인기 있는 아동 문학 작가 중 한 사람입니다. 그는 1954년 미국 뉴욕에서 태어났으며 초등학교 보조 교사로 일한 경험을 바탕으로 쓴 『웨이사이드 학교(Sideways Stories From Wayside School)』 시리즈로 잘 알려져 있습니다. 그 외에도 그는 『마빈 레드포스트(Marvin Redpost)』 시리즈, 『There's a Boy in the Girls' Bathroom(여자화장실에 남자가 있다고?)』, 『The Boy Who Lost His Face(얼굴을 잃어버린 소년)』 등 20여 권의 어린이책을 썼습니다. 그가 1998년에 발표한 『Holes』는 독자들의 큰 사랑을 받으며 National Book Award 등 많은 상을 수상하였고, 마침내 1999년에는 뉴베리 메달을 수상하였습니다. 2006년에는 『Holes』의 후속편 『Small Steps』를 출간하였습니다. 그는 현재 텍사스에서 딸과 아내와 함께 살고 있습니다.

『The Boy Who Lost His Face』는 인기가 많은 친구들과 어울리고 싶어하는 David의 이야기를 담고 있습니다. David는 어느 날 친구들과 함께 동네에서 마녀로 소문난 Bayfield 할머니의 지팡이를 훔치게 됩니다. 그러나 할머니 집에서 빠져 나오려고 할 때, 그에게 Bayfield 할머니는 무시무시한 '저주'를 내립니다. David는 그 저주를 믿지 않았지만 그의 삶은 자꾸 꼬여만 갑니다. 그토록 어울리고 싶었던 친구들은 자기를 놀려대고 스페인어 수업에 바지 지퍼를 내린 채 들어갔다가 학교의 웃음거리가 되어버립니다. 그리고 몰래 마음 속으로 좋아하던 여자아이에게 용기를 내 고백하려는 순간 저주가 그의 발목을 붙잡고 맙니다. 정말로 Bayfield 할머니는 마녀이고 David는 저주에 걸린 것일까요? David는 이 저주를 풀 수 있을까요?
이 작품은 저주에 걸렸다고 믿게 되는 한 소년을 통해 진정한 친구 관계와 올바른 행동을 하는 것의 어려움, 그리고 사춘기 소년의 복잡한 감정을 보여주고 있습니다. 작가 루이스 새커의 치밀하면서도 재치 있는 구성이 돋보이는 작품입니다.

원서 본문

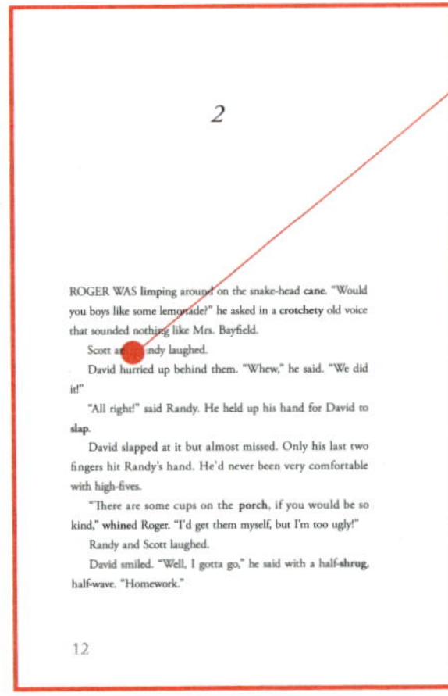

2

ROGER WAS limping around on the snake-head **cane**. "Would you boys like some lemonade?" he asked in a **crotchety** old voice that sounded nothing like Mrs. Bayfield.

Scott and Randy laughed.

David hurried up behind them. "Whew," he said. "We did it!"

"All right!" said Randy. He held up his hand for David to **slap**.

David slapped at it but almost missed. Only his last two fingers hit Randy's hand. He'd never been very comfortable with high-fives.

"There are some cups on the **porch**, if you would be so kind," **whin**ed Roger. "I'd get them myself, but I'm too ugly!"

Randy and Scott laughed.

David smiled. "Well, I gotta go," he said with a half-**shrug**, half-wave. "Homework."

12

내용이 담긴 원서 본문입니다.

원어민이 읽는 일반 원서와 같은 텍스트지만, 암기해야 할 중요 어휘들은 볼드체로 표시되어 있습니다. 이 어휘들은 지금 들고 계신 워크북에 챕터별로 정리되어 있습니다.

학습 심리학 연구 결과에 따르면, 한 단어씩 따로 외우는 단어 암기는 거의 효과가 없다고 합니다. 단어를 제대로 외우기 위해서는 문맥(context) 속에서 단어를 암기해야 하며, 한 단어당 문맥 속에서 15번 이상 마주칠 때 완벽하게 암기할 수 있다고 합니다.

이 책의 본문에서는 중요 어휘를 볼드체로 강조하여, 문맥 속의 단어들을 더 확실히 인지(word cognition in context)하도록 돕고 있습니다. 또한 대부분의 중요 단어들은 다른 챕터에서도 반복해서 등장하기 때문에 이 책을 읽는 것만으로도 자연스럽게 어휘력을 향상시킬 수 있습니다.

또한 본문 하단에는 내용 이해를 돕기 위한 '각주'가 첨가되어 있습니다. 각주는 굳이 암기할 필요는 없지만, 알아 두면 도움이 될 만한 정보를 설명하고 있습니다. 각주를 참고하면 스토리를 더 깊이 있게 이해할 수 있어 원서를 읽는 재미가 배가됩니다.

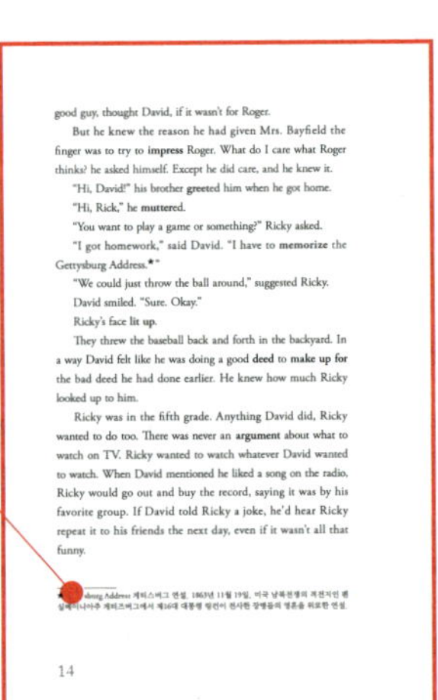

good guy, thought David, if it wasn't for Roger.

But he knew the reason he had given Mrs. Bayfield the finger was to try to **impress** Roger. What do I care what Roger thinks? he asked himself. Except he did care, and he knew it.

"Hi, David!" his brother **greeted** him when he got home.

"Hi, Rick," he **muttered**.

"You want to play a game or something?" Ricky asked.

"I got homework," said David. "I have to **memorize** the Gettysburg Address.*"

"We could just throw the ball around," suggested Ricky.

David smiled. "Sure. Okay."

Ricky's face **lit up**.

They threw the baseball back and forth in the backyard. In a way David felt like he was doing a good **deed** to **make up for** the bad deed he had done earlier. He knew how much Ricky looked up to him.

Ricky was in the fifth grade. Anything David did, Ricky wanted to do too. There was never an **argument** about what to watch on TV. Ricky wanted to watch whatever David wanted to watch. When David mentioned he liked a song on the radio, Ricky would go out and buy the record, saying it was by his favorite group. If David told Ricky a joke, he'd hear Ricky repeat it to his friends the next day, even if it wasn't all that funny.

* Gettysburg Address 게티스버그 연설. 1863년 11월 19일, 미국 남북전쟁의 격전지인 펜실베이니아주 게티스버그에서 제16대 대통령 링컨이 전사한 장병들의 영혼을 위로한 연설.

14

워크북(Workbook)

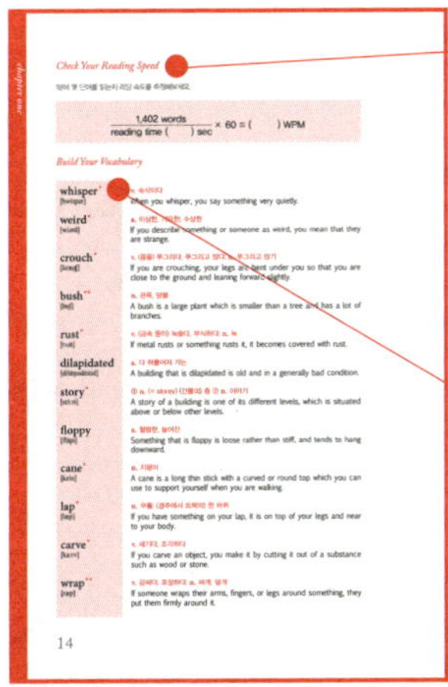

Check Your Reading Speed

해당 챕터의 단어 수가 기록되어 있어, 리딩 속도를 측정할 수 있습니다. 특히 리딩 속도를 중시하는 독자들이 유용하게 사용할 수 있습니다

Build Your Vocabulary

본문에 볼드 표시되어 있는 단어들이 정리되어 있습니다. 리딩 전·후에 반복해서 보면 원서를 더욱 쉽게 읽을 수 있고, 어휘력도 빠르게 향상될 것입니다.

단어는 〈스펠링 – 빈도 – 발음기호 – 품사 – 한글 뜻 – 영문 뜻〉 순서로 표기되어 있으며 빈도 표시(★)가 많을수록 필수 어휘입니다. 반복해서 등장하는 단어는 빈도 대신 '복습'으로 표기되어 있습니다. 품사는 아래와 같이 표기했습니다.

n. 명사 | **a.** 형용사 | **ad.** 부사 | **v.** 동사

conj. 접속사 | **prep.** 전치사 | **int.** 감탄사 | **idiom** 숙어 및 관용구

Comprehension Quiz

간단한 퀴즈를 통해 읽은 내용에 대한 이해력을 점검해 볼 수 있습니다.

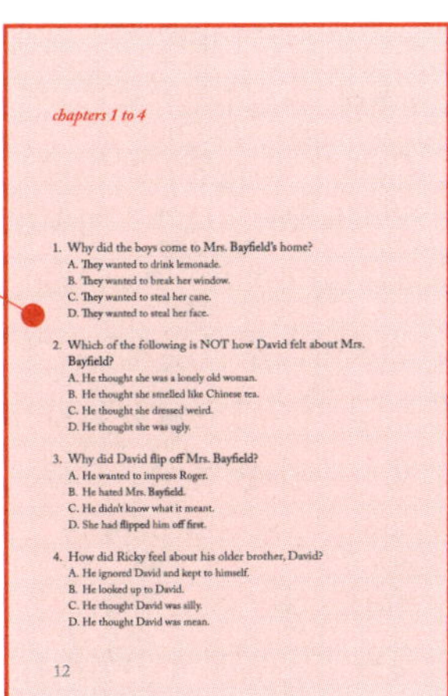

「뉴베리 컬렉션」 이렇게 읽어 보세요!

아래와 같이 프리뷰(Preview) → 리딩(Reading) → 리뷰(Review) 세 단계를 거치면서 읽으면, 더욱 효과적으로 영어 실력을 향상할 수 있습니다.

1. 프리뷰(Preview) : 오늘 읽을 내용을 먼저 점검하자!

- 워크북을 통해 오늘 읽을 챕터에 나와 있는 단어들을 쭉 훑어봅니다. 어떤 단어들이 나오는지, 내가 아는 단어와 모르는 단어는 어떤 것들이 있는지 가벼운 마음으로 살펴봅니다.
- 평소처럼 하나하나 쓰면서 암기하려고 하지는 마세요! 익숙하지 않은 단어들을 주의 깊게 보되, 어차피 리딩을 하면서 점차 익숙해질 단어라는 것을 기억하며 빠르게 훑어봅니다.
- 뒤 챕터로 갈수록 '복습'이라고 표시된 단어들이 늘어나는 것을 알 수 있습니다. '복습' 단어인데도 여전히 익숙하지 않다면 더욱 신경을 써서 봐야겠죠? 매일매일 꾸준히 읽는다면, 익숙한 단어들이 점점 많아진다는 것을 몸으로 느낄 수 있습니다.

2. 리딩(Reading) : 내용에 집중하며 빠르게 읽어 나가자!

- 프리뷰를 마친 후 바로 리딩을 시작합니다. 방금 살펴봤던 어휘들을 문장 속에서 다시 만나게 되는데, 이 과정에서 단어의 쓰임새와 어감을 자연스럽게 익히게 됩니다.
- 모르는 단어나 이해되지 않는 문장이 나오더라도 멈추지 말고 전체적인 맥락을 파악하면서 속도감 있게 읽어 나가세요. 이해되지 않는 문장들은 따로 표시를 하되, 일단 넘어가고 계속 읽는 것이 좋습니다. 뒷부분을 읽다 보면 자연히 이해가 되는 경우도 있고, 정 이해가 되지 않는 부분은 리딩을 마친 이후에 따로 리뷰하는 시간을 가지면 됩니다. 문제집을 풀듯이 모든 문장을 분석하면서 원서를 읽는 것이 아니라, 리딩을 할 때는 리딩에만, 리뷰를 할 때는 리뷰에만 집중하는 것이 필요합니다.
- 볼드 처리된 단어의 의미가 궁금하더라도 워크북을 바로 펼치지 마세요. 정 궁금하다면 한 번씩 참고하는 것도 나쁘진 않지만, 워크북과 원서를 번갈아 보면서 읽는 것은 리딩의 흐름을 끊고 단어 하나하나에 집착하는 좋지 않은 리딩 습관을 심어 줄 수 있습니다.
- 같은 맥락에서 번역서를 구해 원서와 동시에 번갈아 보는 것도 좋은 방법이 아닙니다. 한글 번역을 가지고 있다고 해도 일단 영어로 읽을 때는 영어에만 집중하고 어느 정도 분량을 읽은 후에 번역서와 비교하도록 하세요. 모든 문장을

일일이 번역해서 완벽하게 이해하려는 것은 오히려 좋지 않은 리딩 습관을 심어 주어 장기적으로는 바람직하지 않은 결과를 얻을 수 있습니다. 처음부터 완벽하게 이해하려고 하는 것보다는 빠른 속도로 2~3회 반복해서 읽는 방식이 실력 향상에 더 도움이 됩니다. 만일 반복해서 읽어도 내용이 전혀 이해되지 않아 곤란하다면 책 선정에 문제가 있다고 할 수 있습니다. 그럴 때는 좀 더 쉬운 책을 골라 실력을 다진 뒤 다시 도전하는 것이 좋습니다.

- 초보자라면 분당 150단어의 리딩 속도를 목표로 잡고 리딩을 합니다. 분당 150단어는 원어민이 말하는 속도로, 영어 학습자들이 리스닝과 스피킹으로 넘어가기 위해 가장 기초적으로 달성해야 하는 단계입니다. 분당 50~80단어 정도의 낮은 리딩 속도를 가지고 있는 경우는 대부분 영어 실력이 부족해서라기보다 '잘못된 리딩 습관'을 가지고 있어서 그렇습니다. 이해력이 조금 떨어진다고 하더라도 분당 150단어까지는 속도에 대한 긴장감을 놓치지 말고 속도감 있게 읽어 나가도록 하세요.

3. 리뷰(Review) : 이해력을 점검하고 꼼꼼하게 다시 살펴보자!

- 해당 챕터의 Comprehension Quiz를 통해 이해력을 점검해 봅니다.
- 오늘 만난 어휘들을 다시 한번 복습합니다. 이때는 읽으면서 중요하다고 생각했던 단어를 연습장에 써 보면서 꼼꼼하게 외우는 것도 좋습니다.
- 이해가 되지 않는다고 표시해 두었던 부분도 주의 깊게 분석해 봅니다. 다시 한번 문장을 꼼꼼히 읽고, 어떤 이유에서 이해가 되지 않았는지 생각해 봅니다. 따로 메모를 남기거나 노트를 작성하는 것도 좋은 방법입니다.
- 사실 꼼꼼히 리뷰하는 것은 매우 고된 과정입니다. 원서를 읽고 리뷰하는 시간을 가지는 것이 영어 실력 향상에 많은 도움이 되기는 하지만, 이 과정을 철저히 지키려다가 원서 읽기의 재미를 반감시키는 것은 바람직하지 않습니다. 그럴 때는 차라리 리뷰를 가볍게 하는 것이 좋을 수 있습니다. '내용에 빠져서 재미있게', 문제집에서는 상상도 못할 '많은 양'을 읽으면서, 매일매일 조금씩 꾸준히 실력을 키워 가는 것이 원서를 활용하는 기본적인 방법이며, 영어 공부의 왕도입니다. 문제집 풀듯이 원서 읽기를 시도하고 접근해서는 실패할 수밖에 없습니다.
- 이런 방식으로 원서를 끝까지 다 읽었다면, 다시 반복해서 읽거나 오디오북을 활용하는 등 다양한 방식으로 원서 읽기를 확장해 나갈 수 있습니다. 이에 대한 자세한 안내가 워크북 말미에 실려 있습니다.

1. Why did the boys come to Mrs. Bayfield's home?
   A. They wanted to drink lemonade.
   B. They wanted to break her window.
   C. They wanted to steal her cane.
   D. They wanted to steal her face.

2. Which of the following is NOT how David felt about Mrs. Bayfield?
   A. He thought she was a lonely old woman.
   B. He thought she smelled like Chinese tea.
   C. He thought she dressed weird.
   D. He thought she was ugly.

3. Why did David flip off Mrs. Bayfield?
   A. He wanted to impress Roger.
   B. He hated Mrs. Bayfield.
   C. He didn't know what it meant.
   D. She had flipped him off first.

4. How did Ricky feel about his older brother, David?
   A. He ignored David and kept to himself.
   B. He looked up to David.
   C. He thought David was silly.
   D. He thought David was mean.

5. How did David feel about his mother's reaction to the broken window?
    A. He was glad that he didn't get in trouble.
    B. He thought it was unfair that Ricky got in trouble.
    C. He thought that he should have been punished.
    D. He was upset that he couldn't play anymore.

6. What did David do on his way to school every morning?
    A. He stopped by a fast food restaurant to get breakfast.
    B. He stopped by Scott's house to walk together.
    C. He stopped by Ricky's school to drop him off.
    D. He stopped by the library to drop off books.

7. What did the teacher, Mr. MacFarland, make David do during class?
    A. He made David recite the Gettysburg Address.
    B. He made David stay behind to clean the floor.
    C. He made David sit in a corner of the classroom.
    D. He made David stay down when he fell.

1분에 몇 단어를 읽는지 리딩 속도를 측정해보세요.

$$\frac{1,402 \text{ words}}{\text{reading time ( ) sec}} \times 60 = (\qquad) \text{ WPM}$$

Build Your Vocabulary

whisper[*]
[hwíspər]

v. 속삭이다
When you whisper, you say something very quietly.

weird[*]
[wiərd]

a. 이상한, 기묘한; 수상한
If you describe something or someone as weird, you mean that they are strange.

crouch[*]
[krauʧ]

v. (몸을) 쭈그리다, 쭈그리고 앉다; n. 쭈그리고 앉기
If you are crouching, your legs are bent under you so that you are close to the ground and leaning forward slightly.

bush[**]
[buʃ]

n. 관목, 덤불
A bush is a large plant which is smaller than a tree and has a lot of branches.

rust[*]
[rʌst]

v. (금속 등이) 녹슬다, 부식하다; n. 녹
If metal rusts or something rusts it, it becomes covered with rust.

dilapidated
[dilǽpədèitid]

a. 다 허물어져 가는
A building that is dilapidated is old and in a generally bad condition.

story[*]
[stɔ́:ri]

① n. (= storey) (건물의) 층 ② n. 이야기
A story of a building is one of its different levels, which is situated above or below other levels.

floppy
[flápi]

a. 헐렁한, 늘어진
Something that is floppy is loose rather than stiff, and tends to hang downward.

cane[*]
[kein]

n. 지팡이
A cane is a long thin stick with a curved or round top which you can use to support yourself when you are walking.

lap[*]
[læp]

n. 무릎; (경주에서 트랙의) 한 바퀴
If you have something on your lap, it is on top of your legs and near to your body.

carve[*]
[ka:rv]

v. 새기다, 조각하다
If you carve an object, you make it by cutting it out of a substance such as wood or stone.

wrap[**]
[ræp]

v. 감싸다; 포장하다; n. 싸개, 덮개
If someone wraps their arms, fingers, or legs around something, they put them firmly around it.

embed
[imbéd]

v. (단단히) 박다, 끼워 넣다
If an object embeds itself in a substance or thing, it becomes fixed there firmly and deeply.

stick out

idiom 불쑥 나오다, 돌출하다
If something sticks out, it is further out than something else.

figure out

idiom ~을 생각해내다; 계산하다
If you figure out a solution to a problem or the reason for something, you succeed in solving it or understanding it.

know better than to do something

idiom (~할 정도로) 어리석지는 않다
If someone knows better than to do something, they are old enough or experienced enough to know it is the wrong thing to do.

signal**
[sígnəl]

n. (동작 · 소리로 하는) 신호; v. (동작 · 소리로) 신호를 보내다
A signal is a gesture, sound, or action which is intended to give a particular message to the person who sees or hears it.

grab*
[græb]

v. 붙잡다, 움켜잡다; n. 움켜잡으려고 함
If you grab something, you take it or pick it up suddenly and roughly.

nod**
[nad]

v. (고개를) 끄덕이다; n. (고개를) 끄덕임
If you nod, you move your head downward and upward to show agreement, understanding, or approval.

warn***
[wɔːrn]

v. 경고하다, 주의를 주다, 조심하라고 하다
If you warn someone about something such as a possible danger or problem, you tell them about it so that they are aware of it.

witch*
[witʃ]

n. 마녀
In fairy stories, a witch is a woman, usually an old woman, who has evil magic powers.

snicker
[sníkər]

v. 킬킬 웃다, 숨죽여 웃다; n. 킬킬 웃음
If you snicker, you laugh quietly in a disrespectful way, for example at something rude or embarrassing.

abrupt*
[əbrʌpt]

a. 갑작스러운, 뜻밖의; 퉁명스러운 (abruptly ad. 갑자기)
An abrupt change or action is very sudden, often in a way which is unpleasant.

give someone a dirty look

idiom ~를 째려 보다, 화난 표정을 하다
If someone gives you a dirty look, they look at you in a way which shows that they are angry with you.

peel*
[piːl]

v. 껍질을 벗기다; n. (과일 · 채소의 두꺼운) 껍질
If you peel off something that has been sticking to a surface or if it peels off, it comes away from the surface.

attic*
[ǽtik]

n. 다락(방)
An attic is a room at the top of a house just below the roof.

roof**
[ruːf]

n. 지붕
The roof of a building is the covering on top of it that protects the people and things inside from the weather.

nonsense[**]
[nánsəns]

n. 터무니없는 생각[말], 허튼소리
If you say that something spoken or written is nonsense, you mean that you consider it to be untrue or silly.

get in with

idiom (이익을 바라고) ~에게 친하게 굴다, ~와 친해지다
If you get in with someone, you try to become friendly with them, especially in order to gain an advantage for yourself.

hold back

idiom (진전 · 발전을) 방해하다, 저지하다
If you hold someone or something back, you prevent the progress or development of them.

hang around with someone

idiom ~와 많이 어울리다
If you hang around with someone, you spend a lot of time with them.

stuff[*]
[stʌf]

n. 것(들), 물건, 물질; **v.** 채워 넣다, 속을 채우다
You can use stuff to refer to things such as a substance, a collection of things, events, or ideas, or the contents of something in a general way without mentioning the thing itself by name.

jerk[*]
[dʒəːrk]

① **n.** 바보, 멍청이 ② **v.** 홱 움직이다; **n.** (갑자기 날카롭게) 홱 움직임
If you call someone a jerk, you are insulting them because you think they are stupid or you do not like them.

ignore[**]
[ignɔ́ːr]

v. 무시하다
If you ignore someone or something, you pay no attention to them.

tag along

idiom (청하거나 초대하지 않는데도) (~를) 따라가다
If you tag along, you go somewhere with someone, especially when you have not been invited.

overgrown
[òuvərgróun]

a. (풀 · 잡초 등이) 마구 자란; 너무 커진
If a garden or other place is overgrown, it is covered with a lot of untidy plants because it has not been looked after.

weed[*]
[wiːd]

n. 잡초
A weed is a wild plant that grows in gardens or fields of crops and prevents the plants that you want from growing properly.

rectangle[*]
[réktæŋgl]

n. 직사각형 (rectangular **a.** 직사각형의)
A rectangle is a four-sided shape whose corners are all ninety degree angles. Each side of a rectangle is the same length as the one opposite to it.

patch[*]
[pætʃ]

n. (주변과는 다른 조그만) 부분; (덧대는 데 쓰이는) 조각
A patch on a surface is a part of it which is different in appearance from the area around it.

porch[*]
[pɔːrtʃ]

n. (건물 입구에 지붕이 얹혀 있고 벽이 둘러진) 현관
A porch is a sheltered area at the entrance to a building, which has a roof and sometimes has walls.

pitcher[*]
[pítʃər]

① **n.** 물 주전자 ② **n.** 투수, 피처
A pitcher is a jug.

flush[*]
[flʌʃ]

v. (얼굴 등을) 붉히다; (변기의) 물을 내리다; n. (볼 등의) 홍조
If you flush, your face goes red because you are hot or ill, or because you are feeling a strong emotion such as embarrassment or anger.

shrug[*]
[ʃrʌg]

v. (양 손바닥을 내보이면서 어깨를) 으쓱하다; n. (어깨를) 으쓱하기
If you shrug, you raise your shoulders to show that you are not interested in something or that you do not know or care about something.

mutter[*]
[mʌ́tər]

v. 중얼거리다; 투덜거리다; n. 중얼거림
If you mutter, you speak very quietly so that you cannot easily be heard, often because you are complaining about something.

stomp
[stamp]

v. 쿵쿵거리며 걷다, 발을 구르다
If you stomp somewhere, you walk there with very heavy steps, often because you are angry.

flower bed
[fláuər bèd]

n. 화단
A flower bed is an area of ground in a garden or park which has been specially prepared so that flowers can be grown in it.

crush[**]
[krʌʃ]

v. 짓밟다; 부서지다; (정신 · 희망을) 꺾다; n. 눌러 터뜨림
To crush something means to press it very hard so that its shape is destroyed or so that it breaks into pieces.

sour[**]
[sauər]

a. (맛이) 신, 시큼한
Something that is sour has a sharp, unpleasant taste like the taste of a lemon.

all the way

idiom 완전히; 내내
You can use all the way to emphasize that your remark applies to every part of a situation, activity, or period of time.

sputter
[spʌ́tə:r]

n. 탁탁 하는 소리; v. (엔진 · 불길 등이) 털털거리는 소리를 내다
A sputter is a quick explosive sound.

stare[*]
[stɛər]

v. 빤히 쳐다보다, 응시하다; n. 빤히 쳐다보기, 응시
If you stare at someone or something, you look at them for a long time.

underpants
[ʌ́ndərpænts]

n. 팬티
Underpants are a piece of underwear which have two holes to put your legs through and elastic around the top to hold them up round your waist or hips.

ruffle
[rʌfl]

n. (옷의 목 · 손목 부분에 대는) 주름 장식; v. (반반한 표면을) 헝클다
Ruffles are folds of cloth at the neck or the ends of the arms of a piece of clothing, or are sometimes sewn on things as a decoration.

extend[**]
[ikstén d]

v. 넓어지다, 퍼지다; (손 · 발 등을) 뻗다, 늘이다
If an object extends from a surface or place, it sticks out from it.

hurl[*]
[hə:rl]

v. 세게 내던지다, 집어던지다
If you hurl something, you throw it violently and with a lot of force.

crash[**]
[kræʃ]

v. 충돌하다, 부딪치다; n. (무엇이 떨어지거나 부서질 때 나는) 요란한 소리, 굉음
If something crashes somewhere, it moves and hits something else violently, making a loud noise.

yell[*]
[jel]

v. 소리치다, 고함치다; n. 고함소리, 부르짖음
If you yell, you shout loudly, usually because you are excited, angry, or in pain.

curse[*]
[kə:rs]

n. 저주; 욕(설), 악담; v. 욕(설)을 하다; 저주를 내리다
If you say that there is a curse on someone, you mean that there seems to be a supernatural power causing unpleasant things to happen to them.

slide[*]
[sláid]

v. (slid–slid) 미끄러지다, 미끄러지듯 움직이다
If you slide somewhere, you move there smoothly and quietly.

prop
[prap]

v. (받침대 등으로) 받치다; n. 지주, 버팀목, 받침대
If you prop an object on or against something, you support it by putting something underneath it or by resting it somewhere.

flip someone off

idiom 손가락으로 욕을 하다
If you flip someone off, you raise your middle finger to them in a very rude sign.

flash[**]
[flæʃ]

v. (분노 등으로) 발끈하다; (잠깐) 비치다, 번쩍이다; 비추다; n. 섬광, 번쩍임
If someone's eyes flash, they suddenly show a strong emotion, especially anger.

crackle[*]
[krækl]

v. (타오르는 불이 내는 소리와 같이) 탁탁[치직] 소리를 내다;
n. (짧고 날카롭게) 탁탁[치직] 하는 소리
If something crackles, it makes a rapid series of short, harsh noises.

regurgitate
[rigə:rdʒətèit]

v. (삼킨 음식물을 입 안으로 다시) 역류시키다;
(듣거나 읽은 내용을 별 생각 없이) 반복하다
If a person or animal regurgitates food, they bring it back up from their stomach before it has been digested.

1분에 몇 단어를 읽는지 리딩 속도를 측정해보세요.

$$\frac{1{,}264 \text{ words}}{\text{reading time (}\quad\text{) sec}} \times 60 = (\quad) \text{ WPM}$$

Build Your Vocabulary

limp
[limp]

v. 다리를 절다, 절뚝거리다; **a.** 기운이 없는, 축 처진
If a person or animal limps, they walk with difficulty or in an uneven way because one of their legs or feet is hurt.

cane 복습
[kein]

n. 지팡이
A cane is a long thin stick with a curved or round top which you can use to support yourself when you are walking.

crotchety
[krátʃəti]

a. (쉽게) 짜증을 내는
A crotchety person is bad-tempered and easily irritated.

slap *
[slæp]

v. 찰싹 때리다; 털썩[탁] 놓다; **n.** 찰싹 (때림)
If you slap someone, you hit them with the palm of your hand.

porch 복습
[pɔːrtʃ]

n. (건물 입구에 지붕이 얹혀 있고 벽이 둘러진) 현관
A porch is a sheltered area at the entrance to a building, which has a roof and sometimes has walls.

whine
[hwain]

v. 징징거리다, 우는 소리를 하다
If something or someone whines, they make a long, high-pitched noise, especially one which sounds sad or unpleasant.

shrug 복습
[ʃrʌg]

n. (양 손바닥을 내보이면서 어깨를) 으쓱하기; **v.** (어깨를) 으쓱하다
Shrug is the action of raising and lowering your shoulders to express something.

reply ***
[riplái]

v. 대답하다; 답장을 보내다; **n.** 대답; 답장, 답신
When you reply to something that someone has said or written to you, you say or write an answer to them.

miserable *
[mízərəbl]

a. 비참한
If you are miserable, you are very unhappy.

flip someone off 복습

idiom 손가락으로 욕을 하다
If you flip someone off, you raise your middle finger to them in a very rude sign.

pinky
[píŋki]

n. (= pinkie) 새끼손가락
Your pinky is the smallest finger on your hand.

give someone the finger [bird]

idiom 가운데 손가락을 들어 보이며 모욕하다
If you give someone the finger, you make a rude sign at them with your middle finger.

pretend***
[priténd]

v. ~인 체하다, 가장하다; **a.** 가짜의, 꾸민
If you pretend that something is the case, you act in a way that is intended to make people believe that it is the case, although in fact it is not.

impress*
[imprés]

v. ~에게 (깊은) 인상을 주다; 감동시키다
If something impresses you, you feel great admiration for it.

greet**
[gri:t]

v. 맞다, 환영하다
When you greet someone, you say 'Hello' or shake hands with them.

mutter^{복습}
[mʌ́tər]

v. 중얼거리다; 투덜거리다; **n.** 중얼거림
If you mutter, you speak very quietly so that you cannot easily be heard, often because you are complaining about something.

memorize*
[méməràiz]

v. 암기하다
If you memorize something, you learn it so that you can remember it exactly.

light up

idiom (기쁘거나 신이 나서 두 눈·얼굴이) 환해지다
If your face light up you suddenly look very surprised or happy.

deed*
[di:d]

n. 행위, 행동; (주택·건물의 소유권을 증명하는) 증서
A deed is something that is done, especially something that is very good or very bad.

make up for

idiom ~에 대해 보상하다, (잘못된 상황을 바로잡을 수 있도록) 만회하다
If you make up for something, you do something good for someone because you have treated them badly or because they have done something good for you.

argument**
[á:rgjumənt]

n. 논쟁, 언쟁, 말다툼
An argument is a conversation in which people disagree with each other angrily or noisily.

hardly***
[há:rdli]

ad. 거의 ~아니다, 전혀 ~않다
When you say you can hardly do something, you are emphasizing that it is very difficult for you to do it.

smash*
[smæʃ]

n. 강타; 박살내기; **v.** 박살내다, 부딪치다, 충돌하다
A smash is a powerful downward hit that sends the ball forcefully over the net.

get along with someone

idiom ~와 잘 지내다
If you get along with someone, you be friendly or compatible with them.

idiot
[ídiət]

n. 바보, 멍청이
If you call someone an idiot, you are showing that you think they are very stupid or have done something very stupid.

hang around with someone^{복습}

idiom ~와 많이 어울리다
If you hang around with someone, you spend a lot of time with them.

defenseless
[difénslis]

a. 무방비의
Defenseless people, animals, places, or things are weak and unable to protect themselves from attack.

helpless[*]
[hélplis]

a. 무력한, 속수무책의 (helplessly ad. 무력하게, 어쩔 수 없이)
If you are helpless, you do not have the strength or power to do anything useful or to control or protect yourself.

drag[*]
[dræg]

v. 끌다, 힘들게 움직이다; n. 견인, 끌기
If you drag something, you pull it along the ground.

overgrown[복습]
[òuvərgróun]

a. (풀 · 잡초 등이) 마구 자란; 너무 커진
If a garden or other place is overgrown, it is covered with a lot of untidy plants because it has not been looked after.

crawl[**]
[krɔ:l]

v. 기다, 몹시 느리게 가다; n. 기어가기, 서행
When you crawl, you move forward on your hands and knees.

pitcher[복습]
[pítʃər]

① n. 물 주전자 ② n. 투수, 피처
A pitcher is a jug.

bleed[*]
[bli:d]

v. 피를 흘리다, 출혈하다, 피가 나다
When you bleed, you lose blood from your body as a result of injury or illness.

delight[*]
[diláit]

v. 많은 기쁨을 주다, 아주 즐겁게 하다; n. (큰) 기쁨 (delighted a. 아주 기뻐하는)
If you are delighted, you are extremely pleased and excited about something.

humiliate[*]
[hju:mílièit]

v. 굴욕감을 느끼게 하다, 창피를 주다 (humiliating a. 굴욕적인)
To humiliate someone means to say or do something which makes them feel ashamed or stupid.

clumsy[*]
[klʌ́mzi]

a. 어설픈, 서투른
A clumsy person moves or handles things in a careless, awkward way, often so that things are knocked over or broken.

crippled
[kripld]

a. 다리를 저는, 절름발이인
If someone is crippled by an injury, it is so serious that they can never move their body properly again.

knock[**]
[nak]

v. 치다, 부수다; (문을) 두드리다, 노크하다
If you knock something, you touch or hit it roughly, especially so that it falls or moves.

beam[*]
[bi:m]

v. 활짝 웃다; n. 빛줄기
If you say that someone is beaming, you mean that they have a big smile on their face because they are happy, pleased, or proud about something.

sigh[*]
[sai]

v. 한숨 쉬다; n. 한숨, 탄식
When you sigh, you let out a deep breath, as a way of expressing feelings such as disappointment, tiredness, or pleasure.

criminal[**]
[krímənl]

n. 범죄자, 범인
A criminal is a person who regularly commits crimes.

a split second

idiom 눈 깜짝할 사이
A split second is a very short period of time.

tip *
[tip]

v. 기울어지다, 젖히다; n. (뾰족한) 끝
If you tip an object or part of your body or if it tips, it moves into a sloping position with one end or side higher than the other.

ruffle 복습
[rʌfl]

n. (옷의 목 · 손목 부분에 대는) 주름 장식; v. (반반한 표면을) 헝클다
Ruffles are folds of cloth at the neck or the ends of the arms of a piece of clothing, or are sometimes sewn on things as a decoration.

sail **
[seil]

v. 미끄러지듯 나아가다; 항해하다; n. 돛
If a person or thing sails somewhere, they move there smoothly and fairly quickly.

shatter *
[ʃǽtər]

v. 산산조각이 나다; 파괴하다; n. 파편, 부서진 조각
If something shatters or is shattered, it breaks into a lot of small pieces.

1분에 몇 단어를 읽는지 리딩 속도를 측정해보세요.

$$\frac{402 \text{ words}}{\text{reading time } (\quad) \text{ sec}} \times 60 = (\quad) \text{ WPM}$$

Build Your Vocabulary

caboose
[kəbúːs]

n. (기차의) 승무원실
A caboos is a small train carriage, usually at the back of a train, in which the guard travels.

crash^{복습}
[kræʃ]

v. 충돌하다, 부딪치다; **n.** (무엇이 떨어지거나 부서질 때 나는) 요란한 소리, 굉음
If something crashes somewhere, it moves and hits something else violently, making a loud noise.

bounce[*]
[bauns]

v. 튀다, 튀게 하다; 급히 움직이다, 뛰어다니다; **n.** 튐, 바운드
If something bounces off a surface or is bounced off it, it reaches the surface and is reflected back.

lap^{복습}
[læp]

n. 무릎; (경주에서 트랙의) 한 바퀴
If you have something on your lap, it is on top of your legs and near to your body.

rush^{**}
[rʌʃ]

v. 급히 움직이다, 서두르다; **n.** 혼잡
If you rush somewhere, you go there quickly.

confine[*]
[kənfáin]

v. (활동 · 주제 · 지역 등을) 국한시키다; (좁은 장소나 폐쇄된 곳에) 넣다
If something is confined to a particular place, it exists only in that place.

bedspread
[bédsprèd]

n. (장식용) 침대보
A bedspread is a decorative cover which is put over a bed, on top of the sheets and blankets.

responsibility^{**}
[rispànsəbíləti]

n. 책임(감), 책무
If you have responsibility for something or someone, or if they are your responsibility, it is your job or duty to deal with them and to take decisions relating to them.

suffer^{***}
[sʌ́fər]

v. (질병 · 고통 · 슬픔 · 결핍 등에) 시달리다, 고통받다
If you suffer pain, you feel it in your body or in your mind.

consequence[*]
[kánsəkwèns]

n. (발생한 일의) 결과
The consequences of something are the results or effects of it.

punish^{***}
[pʌ́niʃ]

v. 처벌하다, 벌주다
To punish someone means to make them suffer in some way because they have done something wrong.

1분에 몇 단어를 읽는지 리딩 속도를 측정해보세요.

$$\frac{\text{1,917 words}}{\text{reading time (\quad) sec}} \times 60 = (\quad) \text{ WPM}$$

Build Your Vocabulary

assume[**]
[əsú:m]

v. 추정하다, 가정하다
If you assume that something is true, you imagine that it is true, sometimes wrongly.

big deal
[bíg dí:l]

int. 그게 무슨 대수라고!; n. 대단한 것, 큰 일
(no big deal **int.** 별일 아니다, 대수롭지 않다)
You can say 'big deal' to someone to show that you are not impressed by something that they consider important or impressive.

embarrass[**]
[imbǽrəs]

v. 당황스럽게 만들다 (embarrassed **a.** 쑥스러운, 어색한)
If something or someone embarrasses you, they make you feel shy or ashamed.

give someone the bird [finger][복습]

idiom 가운데 손가락을 들어 보이며 모욕하다
If you give someone the bird, you make a rude sign at them with your middle finger.

babble
[bæbl]

v. (알아듣기 어렵게) 지껄이다, 횡설수설하다; n. 와글와글, 왁자지껄
If someone babbles, they talk in a confused or excited way.

hardly[복습]
[há:rdli]

ad. 거의 ~아니다, 전혀 ~않다
When you say you can hardly do something, you are emphasizing that it is very difficult for you to do it.

curse[복습]
[kə:rs]

n. 저주; 욕(설), 악담; v. 욕(설)을 하다; 저주를 내리다
If you say that there is a curse on someone, you mean that there seems to be a supernatural power causing unpleasant things to happen to them.

sloppy
[slápi]

a. (물기가 많아서) 질척한; 엉성한, 대충 하는
Something that is sloppy has more liquid than it should be, often in a way that is unpleasant.

approach[**]
[əpróuʧ]

v. 접근하다, 다가오다 n. 접근, 가까움
When you approach something, you get closer to it.

immediately[**]
[imí:diətli]

ad. 곧 바로, 즉시
If something happens immediately, it happens without any delay.

block[***]
[blak]

v. (지나가지 못하게) 막다, 차단하다; n. 사각형 덩어리; 구역, 블록
If you block someone's way, you prevent them from going somewhere or entering a place by standing in front of them.

path[**]
[pæθ]

n. 길, 방향; 작은 길
Your path is the space ahead of you as you move along.

recognize[★★]
[rékəgnàiz]

v. (어떤 사람 · 사물을) 알아보다; (존재 · 진실성을) 인식하다
If you recognize someone or something, you know who that person is or what that thing is.

chuckle[★]
[ʧʌkl]

v. 빙그레[싱긋] 웃다
When you chuckle, you laugh quietly.

budge
[bʌdʒ]

v. 약간 움직이다, 꿈쩍하다
If something will not budge or you cannot budge it, it will not move.

repair[★★]
[ripέər]

n. 수리, 보수; **v.** 수리하다, 보수하다
A repair is something that you do to mend a machine, building, piece of clothing, or other thing that has been damaged or is not working properly.

snicker[복습]
[sníkər]

v. 낄낄 웃다, 숨죽여 웃다; **n.** 낄낄 웃음
If you snicker, you laugh quietly in a disrespectful way, for example at something rude or embarrassing.

pervert
[pərvə́:rt]

n. 변태, 성도착자
If you say that someone is a pervert, you mean that you consider their behavior, especially their sexual behavior, to be immoral or unacceptable.

stand guard

idiom 보초 서다, 감시하다
If you stand guard, you stand near a particular person or place because you are responsible forwatching or protecting them.

a split second[복습]

idiom 눈 깜짝할 사이
A split second is a very short period of time.

disapproval[★]
[dìsəprú:vəl]

n. 반감, 못마땅함
If you feel or show disapproval of something or someone, you feel or show that you do not approve of them.

pimple
[pimpl]

n. 여드름, 뾰루지
Pimples are small raised spots, especially on the face.

scoff
[skɔ:f]

v. 비웃다, 조롱하다
If you scoff at something, you speak about it in a way that shows you think it is ridiculous or inadequate.

lack[★★]
[læk]

n. 부족, 결핍; **v.** ~이 없다, 부족하다
If there is a lack of something, there is not enough of it or it does not exist at all.

combination[★★]
[kàmbənéiʃən]

n. 결합, 화합, 조합; (자물쇠 등을 열 수 있도록 숫자를 조합한 일련의) 번호
A combination of things is a mixture of them.

memorize[복습]
[méməràiz]

v. 암기하다
If you memorize something, you learn it so that you can remember it exactly.

impress[복습]
[imprés]

v. ~에게 (깊은) 인상을 주다; 감동시키다 (impressed **a.** 감명을 받은)
If something impresses you, you feel great admiration for it.

pop[*]
[pap]

v. 불쑥 나타나다; 펑[빵] 하는 소리가 나다; n. 펑[빵] (하고 터지는 소리)
If something pops, it moves quickly and suddenly, especially from a closed space.

put-down
[pút-dàun]

n. 사람을 깔아뭉개는 말
A put-down is something that you say or do to criticize someone or make them appear foolish.

definite[**]
[défənit]

a. 확실한, 확고한; 분명한, 뚜렷한 (definitely ad. 확실히, 명확히)
If something such as a decision or an arrangement is definite, it is firm and clear, and unlikely to be changed.

pang
[pæŋ]

n. (갑자기 격렬하게 일어나는 육체적 · 정신적) 고통, 아픔
A pang is a sudden strong feeling or emotion, for example of sadness or pain.

recite[*]
[risáit]

v. 암송하다, 낭독하다; 죽 말하다
When someone recites a poem or other piece of writing, they say it aloud after they have learned it.

beg[*]
[beg]

v. 간청하다, 애원하다; 구걸하다
You say 'I beg your pardon?' when you want someone to repeat what they have just said because you have not heard or understood it.

spacey
[spéisi]

a. 멍한
You can use spacey to describe things, especially music, which seem strange, especially because they are very modern or like things in a dream.

freckle
[frekl]

n. 주근깨
Freckles are small light brown spots on someone's skin, especially on their face.

daydream[*]
[déidrìːm]

v. 공상에 잠기다; n. 백일몽
If you daydream, you think about pleasant things for a period of time, usually about things that you would like to happen.

meadow[*]
[médou]

n. 목초지
A meadow is a field which has grass and flowers growing in it.

count[***]
[kaunt]

v. 수를 세다, 계산하다; 중요하다; (정식으로) 인정되다; n. 셈, 계산
When you count, you say all the numbers one after another up to a particular number.

take someone off

idiom ~를 (경기 등에서) 떠나게[나가게] 하다
If you take someone off, you remove them from the field and not allow them to continue playing.

fourscore
[fɔːrskɔːr]

a. 80의, 20의 4배의
Fourscore means four times twenty.

command[**]
[kəmǽnd]

v. 명령하다, 지휘하다, 지배하다; n. 명령, 지휘
If someone in authority commands you to do something, they tell you that you must do it.

stare[복습]
[stɛər]

v. 빤히 쳐다보다, 응시하다; n. 빤히 쳐다보기, 응시
If you stare at someone or something, you look at them for a long time.

24

occur[★★]
[əkə́:r]

v. 생각이 떠오르다; 일어나다, 생기다
If a thought or idea occurs to you, you suddenly think of it or realize it.

equal[★★★]
[í:kwəl]

v. (수·양·가치 등이) 같다, ~이다; a. (수·양·가치 등이) 동일한, 동등한, 평등한
If something equals a particular number or amount, it is the same as that amount or the equivalent of that amount.

complicated[★★]
[kámplikèitid]

a. 복잡한
If you say that something is complicated, you mean it has so many parts or aspects that it is difficult to understand or deal with.

meek[★]
[mi:k]

a. 온순한, 온화한 (meekly ad. 유순하게)
If you describe a person as meek, you think that they are gentle and quiet, and likely to do what other people say.

rhyme[★]
[raim]

v. (두 단어나 음절이) 운이 맞다; n. (시의) 운
If one word rhymes with another or if two words rhyme, they have a very similar sound.

ridicule[★]
[rídikjù:l]

v. 비웃다, 조롱하다; n. 조롱, 조소
If you ridicule someone or ridicule their ideas or beliefs, you make fun of them in an unkind way.

site[★]
[sait]

n. (사건 등의) 현장; 위치, 장소
The site of an important event is the place where it happened.

bloody[★]
[blʌ́di]

a. (bloodier-bloodiest) 피비린내 나는, 유혈이 낭자한; 피투성이의
If you describe a situation or event as bloody, you mean that it is very violent and a lot of people are killed.

battlefield
[bǽtlfi:ld]

n. 싸움터, 전장
A battlefield is a place where a battle is fought.

casualty
[kǽʒuəlti]

n. 사상자, 피해자
A casualty is a person who is injured or killed in a war or in an accident.

quiver[★]
[kwívər]

v. 떨다, 떨리다; n. (감정·몸의 일부가) 떨림
If something quivers, it shakes with very small movements.

literature[★★]
[lítərətʃər]

n. 문학, 문학작품
Novels, plays, and poetry are referred to as literature, especially when they are considered to be good or important.

poem[★★]
[póuəm]

n. (한 편의) 시
A poem is a piece of writing in which the words are chosen for their beauty and sound and are carefully arranged, often in short lines which rhyme.

honor[★★★]
[ánər]

v. (~으로) ~에게 영광을 베풀다; n. 존경, 공경; 영광(스러운 것)
To honor someone means to treat them or regard them with special attention and respect.

wound[★★]
[wu:nd]

v. (칼·총과 같은 흉기로) 상체[부상]를 입히다; n. 상처, 부상
If a weapon or something sharp wounds you, it damages your body.

horrible[**]
[hɔ́:rəbl]

a. 끔찍한, 소름 끼치게 싫은; 무서운
You can call something horrible when it causes you to feel great shock, fear, and disgust.

dignity[*]
[dígnəti]

n. 위엄, 품위; 존엄성
If someone behaves or moves with dignity, they are calm, controlled, and admirable.

grace[*]
[greis]

n. 품위; 우아함
If someone behaves with grace, they behave in a pleasant, polite, and dignified way, even when they are upset or being treated unfairly.

befit
[bifít]

v. 걸맞다
If something befits a person or thing, it is suitable or appropriate for them.

occasion[***]
[əkéiʒən]

n. (어떤 일이 일어나는 특정한) 때; (특별한) 행사
An occasion is a time when something happens, or a case of it happening.

sheepish
[ʃí:piʃ]

a. (어리석은 · 잘못된 짓을 하여) 멋쩍어 하는 (sheepishly **ad.** 수줍게, 어색하게)
If you look sheepish, you look slightly embarrassed because you feel foolish or you have done something silly.

flash[복습]
[flæʃ]

v. (잠깐) 비치다, 번쩍이다; 비추다; (분노 등으로) 발끈하다; **n.** 섬광, 번쩍임
If a light flashes or if you flash a light, it shines with a sudden bright light, especially as quick, regular flashes of light.

continent[*]
[kántənənt]

n. 대륙
A continent is a very large area of land, such as Africa or Asia, that consists of several countries.

conceive[*]
[kənsí:v]

v. (생각 · 계획 등을) 마음속으로 품다, 상상하다; (아이를) 가지다
If you conceive a plan or idea, you think of it and work out how it can be done.

liberty[**]
[líbərti]

n. (지배 · 권위 등으로부터의) 자유
Liberty is the freedom to live your life in the way that you want, without interference from other people or the authorities.

dedicate[*]
[dédikèit]

v. (시간 · 노력을) 바치다, 전념하다; (책 · 음악 작품 · 공연을) 헌정하다
If you say that someone has dedicated themselves to something, you approve of the fact that they have decided to give a lot of time and effort to it because they think that it is important.

proposition[*]
[prὰpəzíʃən]

n. 명제, 진술; (사업상의) 제의
A proposition is a statement or an idea which people can consider or discuss to decide whether it is true.

lean[**]
[li:n]

v. ~에 기대다; 기울이다, (몸을) 숙이다
If you lean on or against someone or something, you rest against them so that they partly support your weight.

portion[*]
[pɔ́:rʃən]

n. (더 큰 것의) 부분, 일부; 몫
A portion of something is a part of it.

resting-place
[réstiŋ-plèis]

n. (영혼의) 안식처, 무덤; 휴식처, 휴게소
You can refer to the place where a dead person is buried as their resting-place or their final resting-place.

fitting[*]
[fítiŋ]

a. (어떤 경우에) 어울리는, 적합한
Something that is fitting is right or suitable.

proper[**]
[prápər]

a. 적절한, 제대로 된
The proper thing is the one that is correct or most suitable.

topple
[tapl]

v. 넘어지다; 넘어뜨리다
If someone or something topples somewhere or if you topple them, they become unsteady or unstable and fall over.

in a sense

idiom 어떤 의미에서는
If you say that something is true in a sense, you mean that it is partly true, or true in one way.

consecrate
[kánsəkrèit]

v. (종교적 목적으로) 바치다, 봉헌하다; (종교 의식을 통해) 축성하다
When a building, place, or object is consecrated, it is officially declared to be holy.

hallow
[hǽlou]

v. 신성하게 하다
If you hallow something, you make it holy or set apart for holy use.

flip someone off[복습]

idiom 손가락으로 욕을 하다
If you flip someone off, you raise your middle finger to them in a very rude sign.

vain[*]
[vein]

a. 헛된, 소용없는; 자만심이 강한, 허영심이 많은
If you do something in vain, you do not succeed in achieving what you intend.

perish[*]
[périʃ]

v. 죽다, 소멸되다
If people or animals perish, they die as a result of very harsh conditions or as the result of an accident.

1. How did David feel about shop class?
    A. He would rather have taken home economics.
    B. It was useful for knowing how to cook.
    C. It was his favorite and best class.
    D. He wished that there was a rule that girls couldn't take it.

2. Why did Mo ask David if his project was for his girlfriend?
    A. It was his girlfriend's birthday that day.
    B. It looked like a heart to Mo.
    C. It had his initials carved in it.
    D. It had a girl's name written on it.

3. What reason did Scott give David for not waiting for him in the morning?
    A. He had to practice football early before school.
    B. His new friends gave him a ride in a car.
    C. It wasn't good for his reputation.
    D. David was too slow.

4. Why did pretending to believe he had been cursed make David feel better?
    A. It gave him an excuse that things weren't his fault.
    B. It gave him something exciting to think about.
    C. It made him more popular at school.
    D. It gave him a problem to solve.

5. What reason did David tell his father for why he had flipped off his mother?
    A. He was angry with his mother for not punishing him for the broken window.
    B. He was doing an experiment to see if his mother knew what it meant.
    C. He had been cursed by an evil witch that wanted to ruin his life.
    D. He thought that flipping someone off meant "I love you."

6. Why did David drop Scott's lunch in the trash can?
    A. Scott told him that he was eating out today.
    B. He didn't want Scott to get sick from eating it.
    C. He didn't want to ruin Scott's reputation.
    D. He didn't want to ruin Scott's appetite.

7. What did David want to know about Miss Williams?
    A. He wanted to know her phone number.
    B. He wanted to know her first name.
    C. He wanted to know her address.
    D. He wanted to know her favorite color.

1분에 몇 단어를 읽는지 리딩 속도를 측정해보세요.

$$\frac{878 \text{ words}}{\text{reading time (} \quad \text{) sec}} \times 60 = (\quad) \text{ WPM}$$

Build Your Vocabulary

recess[*]
[risés]

n. (학교의) 쉬는 시간; 휴회
A recess is a short period of time when you have a rest or a change from what you are doing, especially if you are working or if you are in a boring or unpleasant situation.

hang out

idiom 사귀다, 어울리다
If you hang out, you spend a lot of time in a place or with a person or a group of people.

barely[*]
[béərli]

ad. 간신히, 가까스로; 거의 ~않다
You use barely to say that something is only just true or only just the case.

planter
[plǽntər]

n. 화분
A planter is a container for plants that people keep in their homes.

plaster[*]
[plǽstər]

v. 도배를 하다시피 하다; 회반죽을 바르다; n. 회반죽, 석고반죽
If you plaster, you cover a surface or an object with something completely or thickly.

swipe
[swaip]

v. 훔치다, 슬쩍하다; 후려치다, 후려치려고 하다; n. 후려치기
If you swipe something, you steal it quickly.

warn 복습
[wɔːrn]

v. 경고하다, 주의를 주다, 조심하라고 하다
If you warn someone about something such as a possible danger or problem, you tell them about it so that they are aware of it.

mysterious[**]
[mistíəriəs]

a. 신비한, 불가사의한
Someone or something that is mysterious is strange and is not known about or understood.

whisper 복습
[hwíspər]

v. 속삭이다
When you whisper, you say something very quietly.

get away with something

idiom 그럭저럭 해 나가다; (나쁜 짓을 하고도) 처벌을 모면하다
If you get away with something, you do it successfully although it is not the best way of doing it.

draft[*]
[dræft]

v. 제도하다, 밑그림을 그리다; 초안을 작성하다;
n. 원고, 초안 (drafting paper n. 제도용지)
When you draft a letter, book, or speech, you write the first version of it.

maple[*]
[meipl]

n. 단풍나무
A maple or a maple tree is a tree with five-pointed leaves which turn bright red or gold in autumn.

slip*
[slip]

v. (어떤 위치 · 손을 벗어나) 미끄러지다, 빠져 나가다; (재빨리 · 슬며시) 놓다;
n. (작은 종이) 조각, 쪽지
If something slips, it slides out of place or out of your hand.

nail**
[neil]

n. 못; 손톱; 발톱; v. 못으로 박다, 고정하다
A nail is a thin piece of metal with one pointed end and one flat end.
You hit the flat end with a hammer in order to push the nail into
something such as a wall.

fascinate*
[fǽsənèit]

v. 매혹하다, 반하게 하다 (fascinated a. 매혹된, 마음을 빼앗긴)
If something fascinates you, it interests and delights you so much that
your thoughts tend to concentrate on it.

wield
[wi:ld]

v. (무기 · 도구를) 휘두르다; (권력 · 권위 등을) 행사하다
If you wield a weapon, tool, or piece of equipment, you carry and use
it.

pound**
[paund]

① v. 쿵쿵 울리다, 마구 치다, 세게 두드리다; n. 타격 ② n. 파운드(무게의 단위)
③ n. 주인 잃은 개 보호소
If you pound something or pound on it, you hit it with great force,
usually loudly and repeatedly.

all the way복습

idiom 완전히; 내내
You can use all the way to emphasize that your remark applies to
every part of a situation, activity, or period of time.

cautious*
[kɔ́:ʃəs]

a. 조심성 있는, 신중한 (cautiously ad. 조심스럽게)
Someone who is cautious acts very carefully in order to avoid possible
danger.

approach복습
[əpróutʃ]

v. 접근하다, 다가오다 n. 접근, 가까움
When you approach something, you get closer to it.

jig saw
[jíg sɔ:]

n. 실톱; 조각그림 맞추기 (퍼즐)
A jig saw is a tool with an electric motor and a thin metal blade that
is used for cutting curves in flat materials, such as wood or metal.

maneuver
[mənú:vər]

v. (능숙하게 · 조심조심) 움직이다; n. (조심해서 기술적으로 하는) 동작
If you maneuver something into or out of an awkward position, you
skilfully move it there.

vibrate*
[váibreit]

v. (가늘게) 떨다, 흔들리다, 진동하다
If something vibrates or if you vibrate it, it shakes with repeated small,
quick movements.

vertical*
[vɔ́:rtikəl]

a. 수직의, 세로의
Something that is vertical stands or points straight up.

blade*
[bleid]

n. (칼 · 도구 등의) 날; (엔진 · 헬리콥터 등의) 날개깃
The blade of a knife, ax, or saw is the edge, which is used for cutting.

stem**
[stem]

n. (식물의) 줄기
The stem of a plant is the thin, upright part on which the flowers and
leaves grow.

console*
[kənsóul]

v. 위로하다, 위안을 주다
If you console someone who is unhappy about something, you try to
make them feel more cheerful.

sheet** [ʃíːt]	**n.** (종이) 한 장; 시트(침대에 깔거나 위로 덮는 얇은 천) A sheet of paper is a rectangular piece of paper.
shrug 복습 [ʃrʌg]	**v.** (양 손바닥을 내보이면서 어깨를) 으쓱하다; **n.** (어깨를) 으쓱하기 If you shrug, you raise your shoulders to show that you are not interested in something or that you do not know or care about something.
flatter* [flǽtər]	**v.** 자기가 잘난 줄 착각하다; 아첨하다, 알랑거리다 (flattered **a.** 우쭐한) If you are flattered by something that has happened, you are pleased about it because it makes you feel important or special.
carve 복습 [kaːrv]	**v.** 새기다, 조각하다 If you carve an object, you make it by cutting it out of a substance such as wood or stone.
initial*	**n.** (pl.) 성명의 첫 글자[머리글자]들; **a.** 처음의, 초기의 Initials are the capital letters which begin each word of a name. For example, if your full name is Michael Dennis Stocks, your initials will be M.D.S.
bang* [bæŋ]	**v.** 쾅[탕]하고 치다; 쾅 하고 닫다; **n.** 쾅[쿵] (하는 소리) If you bang on something or if you bang it, you hit it hard, making a loud noise.
glance* [glæns]	**v.** 흘긋 보다, 잠깐 보다; **n.** 흘긋 봄 If you glance at something or someone, you look at them very quickly and then look away again immediately.
measly [míːzli]	**a.** 쥐꼬리만한 If you describe an amount, quantity, or size as measly, you are critical of it because it is very small or inadequate.
nod 복습 [nad]	**v.** (고개를) 끄덕이다; **n.** (고개를) 끄덕임 If you nod, you move your head downward and upward to show agreement, understanding, or approval.
ignore 복습 [ignɔ́ːr]	**v.** 무시하다 If you ignore someone or something, you pay no attention to them.
suspicious [səspíʃəs]	**a.** 의심하는, 수상쩍은 (suspiciously **ad.** 의심하듯이, 수상쩍게) If you are suspicious of someone or something, you do not trust them, and are careful when dealing with them.
crack up	**idiom** 마구 웃기 시작하다 If you crack up, you suddenly start laughing a lot.
buzz off	**idiom** 꺼져 You say 'buzz off' to someone, not very politely, to tell them go away.
rabies [réibiːz]	**n.** 광견병 Rabies is a serious disease which causes people and animals to go mad and die. Rabies is particularly common in dogs.
ass* [æs]	**n.** (속어) 엉덩이 Your ass is your bottom.

threaten[**] [θretn]

v. 협박하다, 위협하다
If you do not dare to do something, you do not have enough courage to do it, or you do not want to do it because you fear the consequences.

dare[*] [dɛər]

v. 감히 ~하다, 무릅쓰다, 도전하다
If you dare to do something, you do something which requires a lot of courage.

slam[*] [slæm]

v. 세게[힘껏] 놓다; 쾅[탁] 닫다
If you slam something down, you put it there quickly and with great force.

threaten[**] [θretn]

v. 협박하다, 위협하다
If you do not dare to do something, you do not have enough courage to do it, or you do not want to do it because you fear the consequences.

dare[*] [dɛər]

v. 감히 ~하다, 무릅쓰다, 도전하다
If you slam something down, you put it there quickly and with great force.

1분에 몇 단어를 읽는지 리딩 속도를 측정해보세요.

$$\frac{683 \text{ words}}{\text{reading time (} \quad \text{) sec}} \times 60 = (\quad) \text{ WPM}$$

Build Your Vocabulary

cigarette*
[sìgərét]

n. 담배
Cigarettes are small tubes of paper containing tobacco which people smoke.

reputation*
[rèpjutéiʃən]

n. 명성, 평판
Something's or someone's reputation is the opinion that people have about how good they are.

take a chance

idiom 운에 맡기다, (모험치고) 해보다
When you take a chance, you try to do something although there is a large risk of danger or failure.

backwards*
[bǽkwərdz]

ad. 거꾸로, 반대 방향으로; 뒤로
If you do something backwards, you do it in the opposite way to the usual way.

call on some

idiom (이름을 불러서) ~에게 시키다; (사람을) 방문하다
If you call on someone, you ask someone in a class to answer a question or give their opinion.

recite^{복습}
[risáit]

v. 암송하다, 낭독하다; 죽 말하다
When someone recites a poem or other piece of writing, they say it aloud after they have learned it.

dignity^{복습}
[dígnəti]

n. 위엄, 품위; 존엄성
If someone behaves or moves with dignity, they are calm, controlled, and admirable.

grace^{복습}
[greis]

n. 품위; 우아함
If someone behaves with grace, they behave in a pleasant, polite, and dignified way, even when they are upset or being treated unfairly.

befit^{복습}
[bifít]

v. 걸맞다
If something befits a person or thing, it is suitable or appropriate for them.

occasion^{복습}
[əkéiʒən]

n. (어떤 일이 일어나는 특정한) 때; (특별한) 행사
An occasion is a time when something happens, or a case of it happening.

memorize^{복습}
[méməràiz]

v. 암기하다
If you memorize something, you learn it so that you can remember it exactly.

crack up^{복습}

idiom 마구 웃기 시작하다
If you crack up, you suddenly start laughing a lot.

amazement[*]
[əméizmənt]

n. (대단한) 놀라움
Amazement is the feeling you have when something surprises you very much.

neat[**]
[ni:t]

a. 뛰어난, 훌륭한; 정돈된, 단정한, 말쑥한
If you say that something is neat, you mean that it is very good.

nerd
[nə:rd]

n. 멍청하고 따분한 사람
If you say that someone is a nerd, you mean that they are stupid or ridiculous, especially because they wear unfashionable clothes or show too much interest in computers or science.

so-called[*]
[sóu-kɔːld]

a. 소위, 이른바; 흔히 ~라고 일컬어지는
You use so-called to indicate that you think a word or expression used to describe someone or something is in fact wrong.

put down

idiom (아기를) 재우다; (손에 들고 있던 것을) 내려놓다
If you put down a baby, you place and make it comfortable in the place where it sleeps.

hazel
[héizəl]

a. (눈의 색깔이) 녹갈색[적갈색]인; **n.** 개암나무
Hazel eyes are greenish-brown in color.

worn out

idiom (힘든 노동 · 운동으로) 매우 지친; 닳아서 못 쓰게 된
Someone who is worn out is extremely tired after hard work or a difficult or unpleasant experience.

content[*]
[kəntént]

① **a.** (자기가 가진 것에) 만족하는; **v.** ~에 자족하다
② **n.** (pl.) (어떤 것의) 속에 든 것들, 내용물; 목차
If you are content with something, you are willing to accept it, rather than wanting something more or something better.

statistical[*]
[stətístikəl]

a. 통계적인, 통계학상의, 통계에 근거한
Statistical means relating to the use of statistics.

analysis[*]
[ənǽləsis]

n. 분석 (연구)
Analysis is the process of considering something carefully or using statistical methods in order to understand it or explain it.

occasionally[*]
[əkéiʒənəli]

ad. 가끔
Occasionally means sometimes but not often.

obvious[**]
[ábviəs]

a. 명백한, 분명한 (obviously **ad.** 분명히, 명백하게)
If something is obvious, it is easy to see or understand.

react[*]
[riǽkt]

v. 반응하다, 반응을 보이다
When you react to something that has happened to you, you behave in a particular way because of it.

strained
[streind]

a. 긴장한; 껄끄러운, 불편한
If someone's appearance, voice, or behavior is strained, they seem worried and nervous.

slam[복습]
[slæm]

v. 쾅[탁] 닫다; 세게[힘껏] 놓다
If you slam a door or window or if it slams, it shuts noisily and with great force.

1분에 몇 단어를 읽는지 리딩 속도를 측정해보세요.

$$\frac{1{,}141 \text{ words}}{\text{reading time (} \qquad \text{) sec}} \times 60 = (\qquad) \text{ WPM}$$

Build Your Vocabulary

proper^{복습} [prápər]	**a.** 적절한, 제대로 된 (properly **ad.** 제대로, 적절히) The proper thing is the one that is correct or most suitable.
lab [læb]	**n.** (= laboratory) 실험실, 연구실 A lab is the same as a laboratory, which means a room where scientific experiments, analyses, and research are carried out.
involve** [inválv]	**v.** 참여시키다; (중요 요소로 · 필연적으로) 수반[포함]하다 (involved **a.** 몰두하는, 열중하는) If you are involved in something, you give a lot of time, effort, or attention to it.
experiment*** [ikspérəmənt]	**n.** (과학적인) 실험 An experiment is a scientific test which is done in order to discover what happens to something in particular conditions.
cure** [kjuər]	**n.** 치유하는 약, 치유법; **v.** (사람 · 동물을 아프지 않도록) 낫게 하다 A cure for an illness is a medicine or other treatment that cures the illness.
cancer* [kǽnsər]	**n.** 암 Cancer is a serious disease in which cells in a person's body increase rapidly in an uncontrolled way, producing abnormal growths.
carry away	**idiom** 넋을 잃게 하다, 열중하게 하다 If you are carried away, you are so eager or excited about something that you do something hasty or foolish.
clone [kloun]	**v.** 복제하다; **n.** 클론, 복제 (생물) To clone an animal or plant means to produce exactly same animal or plant artificially, for example in a laboratory, from the cells.
splice [splais]	**v.** (두 끝을) 붙이다, 잇다 If you splice two pieces of rope, film, or tape together, you join them neatly at the ends so that they make one continuous piece.
molecule* [máləkjù:l]	**n.** 분자 A molecule is the smallest amount of a chemical substance which can exist by itself.
grant** [grænt]	**n.** (정부나 단체에서 주는) 보조금; **v.** (공식적 · 법적으로) 승인[허락]하다 A grant is an amount of money that a government or other institution gives to an individual or to an organization for a particular purpose such as education or home improvements.

eventually^{**}
[ivénʧuəli]

ad. 결국, 마침내
Eventually means at the end of a situation or process or as the final result of it.

ashamed^{**}
[əʃéimd]

a. 부끄러워하는
If someone is ashamed, they feel embarrassed or guilty because of something they do or they have done.

give someone the finger [bird]^{복습}

idiom 가운데 손가락을 들어 보이며 모욕하다
If you give someone the finger, you make a rude sign at them with your middle finger.

impress^{복습}
[imprés]

v. ~에게 (깊은) 인상을 주다; 감동시키다
If something impresses you, you feel great admiration for it.

mysterious^{복습}
[mistíəriəs]

a. 신비한, 불가사의한
Someone or something that is mysterious is strange and is not known about or understood.

curse^{복습}
[kə:rs]

n. 저주; 욕(설), 악담; **v.** 욕(설)을 하다; 저주를 내리다
If you say that there is a curse on someone, you mean that there seems to be a supernatural power causing unpleasant things to happen to them.

odd^{**}
[ad]

a. 이상한, 특이한
If you describe someone or something as odd, you think that they are strange or unusual.

pretend^{복습}
[priténd]

v. ~인 체하다, 가장하다; **a.** 가짜의, 꾸민
If you pretend that something is the case, you act in a way that is intended to make people believe that it is the case, although in fact it is not.

tear^{**}
[ter]

① **v.** (tore-torn) 찢다, 찢어지다; **n.** 찢음 ② **n.** 눈물
If you tear paper, cloth, or another material, or if it tears, you pull it into two pieces or you pull it so that a hole appears in it.

curly[*]
[kə́:rli]

a. 곱슬곱슬한
Curly hair is full of curls.

recede
[risí:d]

v. (이마 부분의 머리카락이) 벗어지다; (서서히) 물러나다
If a man's hair starts to recede, it no longer grows on the front of his head.

scraggly
[skrǽgli]

a. 듬성듬성[들쭉날쭉] 자란
Scraggly hair or plants are thin and untidy.

beard[*]
[biərd]

n. (턱)수염
A man's beard is the hair that grows on his chin and cheeks.

mustache[*]
[mʌ́stæʃ]

n. 코밑수염
A man's mustache is the hair that grows on his upper lip.

stare^{복습}
[stɛər]

v. 빤히 쳐다보다, 응시하다; **n.** 빤히 쳐다보기, 응시
If you stare at someone or something, you look at them for a long time.

incredulous
[inkrédʒuləs]

a. 믿지 않는, 못 믿겠다는 듯한 (incredulously ad. 의심하듯이, 수상쩍게 여기듯이)
If someone is incredulous, they are unable to believe something because it is very surprising or shocking.

bend**
[bend]

v. 구부리다, 굽히다, 숙이다; n. 커브, 굽음, 굽은 곳
When you bend, you move the top part of your body downwards and forwards. Plants and trees also bend.

pure**
[pjuər]

a. 순수한, 맑은, 깨끗한
A pure substance is not mixed with anything else.

innocent*
[ínəsənt]

a. 순진한; 잘못이 없는, 결백한
If someone is innocent, they have no experience or knowledge of the more complex or unpleasant aspects of life.

remark**
[rimá:rk]

v. (말이나 글로 의견 · 생각 등을) 발언하다; n. 발언, 언급
If you remark that something is the case, you say that it is the case.

inherent*
[inhíərənt]

a. 내재하는 (inherently ad. 본질적으로)
The inherent qualities of something are the necessary and natural parts of it.

insult*
[insʌ́lt]

n. 모욕(적인 말 · 행동); v. 모욕하다
If someone insults you, they say or do something that is rude or offensive.

mull
[mʌl]

v. 숙고하다, 궁리하다; n. 실수, 실패
If you mull something, you think about it for a long time before deciding what to do.

bother*
[báðər]

v. 신경 쓰다, 애를 쓰다; 귀찮게 하다, 귀찮게 말을 걸다; n. 성가심
If you do not bother to do something or if you do not bother with it, you do not do it, consider it, or use it because you think it is unnecessary or because you are too lazy.

flip someone off복습

idiom 손가락으로 욕을 하다
If you flip someone off, you raise your middle finger to them in a very rude sign.

stroll*
[stroul]

n. (한가로이) 거닐기, 산책; v. 거닐다, 산책하다
If you take for a stroll somewhere, you walk there in a slow, relaxed way.

offend*
[əfénd]

v. 기분을 상하게 하다, 불쾌하게 하다
If you offend someone, you say or do something rude which upsets or embarrasses them.

apologize**
[əpálədʒàiz]

v. 사과하다, 사죄하다
When you apologize to someone, you say that you are sorry that you have hurt them or caused trouble for them.

delight복습
[diláit]

v. 많은 기쁨을 주다, 아주 즐겁게 하다; n. (큰) 기쁨 (delighted a. 아주 기뻐하는)
If you are delighted, you are extremely pleased and excited about something.

flatter복습
[flǽtər]

v. 자기가 잘난 줄 착각하다; 아첨하다, 알랑거리다 (flattered a. 우쭐한)
If you are flattered by something that has happened, you are pleased about it because it makes you feel important or special.

1분에 몇 단어를 읽는지 리딩 속도를 측정해보세요.

$$\frac{899 \text{ words}}{\text{reading time (}\quad\text{) sec}} \times 60 = (\quad\quad) \text{ WPM}$$

Build Your Vocabulary

figure***
[fígjər]

v. (~일 거라고) 생각[판단]하다; 계산하다; **n.** 수치; 숫자
If you figure that something is the case, you think or guess that it is the case.

might as well

idiom ~하는 편이 낫다
If you say that you might as well do something, or that you may as well do it, you mean that you will do it although you do not have a strong desire to do it and may even feel slightly unwilling to do it.

sack*
[sæk]

n. (쇼핑 물건을 담는 크고 튼튼한 종이) 봉지; 부대, 자루
A sack is a paper bag that is used to carry things bought in a food shop.

all the way^{복습}

idiom 완전히; 내내
You can use all the way to emphasize that your remark applies to every part of a situation, activity, or period of time.

trash*
[træʃ]

n. 쓰레기; **v.** 부수다, 엉망으로 만들다 (trash can **n.** 쓰레기통)
Trash consists of unwanted things or waste material such as used paper, empty containers and bottles, and waste food.

ruin**
[ru:in]

v. 망치다, 못쓰게 만들다; 몰락하다; **n.** 파멸, 멸망
To ruin something means to severely harm, damage, or spoil it.

reputation^{복습}
[rèpjutéiʃən]

n. 명성, 평판
Something's or someone's reputation is the opinion that people have about how good they are.

witch^{복습}
[witʃ]

n. 마녀
In fairy stories, a witch is a woman, usually an old woman, who has evil magic powers.

somehow**
[sʌ́mhàu]

ad. 왜 그런지 (모르겠지만), 왠지
You use somehow to say that you do not know or cannot say how something was done or will be done.

weird^{복습}
[wiərd]

a. 이상한, 기묘한; 수상한
If you describe something or someone as weird, you mean that they are strange.

pop^{복습}
[pap]

v. 불쑥 나타나다; 펑[빵] 하는 소리가 나다; **n.** 펑[빵] (하고 터지는 소리)
If something pops, it moves quickly and suddenly, especially from a closed space.

flash ^{복습}
[flæʃ]

v. (잠깐) 비치다, 번쩍이다; 비추다; (분노 등으로) 발끈[폭발]하다 **n.** 섬광, 번쩍임
If a light flashes or if you flash a light, it shines with a sudden bright light, especially as quick, regular flashes of light.

gag
[gæg]

① **v.** 말문을 막다, 재갈을 물리다; **n.** 재갈 ② **n.** 익살, 개그; **v.** 농담하다
If someone gags you, they tie a piece of cloth around your mouth in order to stop you from speaking or shouting.

blush *
[blʌʃ]

v. 얼굴을 붉히다, 얼굴이 빨개지다; **n.** (당황하거나 수치스러워) 얼굴이 붉어짐
When you blush, your face becomes redder than usual because you are ashamed or embarrassed.

nerd ^{복습}
[nəːrd]

n. 멍청하고 따분한 사람 (nerdy **a.** 얼간이 같은)
If you say that someone is a nerd, you mean that they are stupid or ridiculous, especially because they wear unfashionable clothes or show too much interest in computers or science.

dumb *
[dʌm]

a. 멍청한, 바보 같은; 벙어리의, 말을 못 하는
If you call a person dumb, you mean that they are stupid or foolish.

prominent *
[prámənənt]

a. 유명한; 눈에 잘 띄는, 두드러진, 현저한
Someone who is prominent is important.

assassinate *
[əsǽsənèit]

v. 암살하다
When someone important is assassinated, they are murdered as a political act.

fire ***
[faiər]

v. 발사하다; 불을 지르다; 해고하다; **n.** 불, 화재
If someone fires a gun or a bullet, or if they fire, a bullet is sent from a gun that they are using.

pistol *
[pístəl]

n. 권총, 피스톨
A pistol is a small gun which is held in and fired from one hand.

period **
[píːriəd]

n. (학교의 일과를 나눠 놓은) 시간; 기간, 시기; (여성의) 생리
At a school or college, a period is one of the parts that the day is divided into during which lessons or other activities take place.

recess ^{복습}
[risés]

n. (학교의) 쉬는 시간; 휴회
A recess is a short period of time when you have a rest or a change from what you are doing, especially if you are working or if you are in a boring or unpleasant situation.

hang out ^{복습}

idiom 사귀다, 어울리다
If you hang out, you spend a lot of time in a place or with a person or a group of people.

sigh ^{복습}
[sái]

v. 한숨 쉬다; **n.** 한숨, 탄식
When you sigh, you let out a deep breath, as a way of expressing feelings such as disappointment, tiredness, or pleasure.

doubt ***
[daut]

v. 확신하지 못하다, 의심하다; **n.** 의심, 의혹, 의문
If you doubt whether something is true or possible, you believe that it is probably not true or possible.

silky
[sílki]

a. 비단 같은
If something has a silky texture, it is smooth, soft, and shiny, like silk.

blond[*]
[bland]

a. (머리가) 금발인
A woman who has blond hair has pale-colored hair.

attention^{**}
[əténʃən]

n. 주의 (집중), 주목
If you give someone or something your attention, you look at it, listen to it, or think about it carefully.

frizzy
[frízi]

a. (머리가) 곱슬곱슬한
Frizzy hair is very tightly curled.

exclaim[*]
[ikskléim]

v. 외치다, 소리치다
If you exclaim, you say or shout something suddenly because of surprise, fear and pleasure.

glance^{복습}
[glæns]

v. 흘긋 보다, 잠깐 보다; **n.** 흘긋 봄
If you glance at something or someone, you look at them very quickly and then look away again immediately.

out of the corner of one's eye

idiom 곁눈질로
If you see something out of the corner of your eye, you see it not very clearly because you see it from the side of your eye and are not looking straight at it.

1. What did David try to do during P.E. class?
    A. He tried to play volleyball instead.
    B. He tried to score a goal on Roger.
    C. He tried to join Roger's team.
    D. He tried to leave class.

2. Why did David return with the ball happy?
    A. He spoke with Miss Williams.
    B. He scored a goal on Roger.
    C. He won the game for his team.
    D. He was friends with Roger.

3. Why did the class laugh at David during Spanish class?
    A. He made a mistake speaking Spanish.
    B. He forgot his homework.
    C. He had his zipper down.
    D. He was late and missed a quiz.

4. What did Larry promise to bring David the next day?
    A. A dollar
    B. Photos of naked girls
    C. A book about Venezuala
    D. His homework about South America

5. What did David notice about the things happening to him?

    A. They all happened while he was in school.

    B. They were done by someone else to him.

    C. They all happened whenever he thought about Mrs. Bayfield.

    D. They were the same things that happened to Mrs. Bayfield.

6. Which of the following was NOT one of the things that happened to David?

    A. He broke a window.

    B. He fell out of his chair.

    C. He spilled chocolate milk.

    D. He had his zipper down.

7. How did David feel after looking at Larry's photos?

    A. He felt that all of his own problems were insignificant.

    B. He felt that the curse on him had finally been broken.

    C. He felt like moving to Venezuela to live there.

    D. He felt glad to be able to go to school.

1분에 몇 단어를 읽는지 리딩 속도를 측정해보세요.

$$\frac{660 \text{ words}}{\text{reading time (} \quad \text{) sec}} \times 60 = (\quad) \text{ WPM}$$

Build Your Vocabulary

goalie
[góuli]

n. (= goalkeeper) 골키퍼
A goalie is the player in a sports team whose job is to guard the goal.

sweat[*]
[swet]

v. 땀 흘리다; 습기가 차다; **n.** 땀 (sweaty **a.** 땀흘린, 땀범벅인)
When you sweat, drops of liquid comes through your skin.

mess[*]
[mes]

v. 엉망으로 만들다; **n.** (지저분하고) 엉망(진창)인 상태
If you mess something up, you make it untidy.

shin
[ʃin]

n. 정강이
Your shins are the front parts of your legs between your knees and your ankles.

lean[복습]
[li:n]

v. 기울이다, (몸을) 숙이다; ~에 기대다
When you lean in a particular direction, you bend your body in that direction.

casual[**]
[kǽʒuəl]

a. 태평스러운 (듯한), 무심한; 격식을 차리지 않는, 평상시의 (casually **ad.** 무심코)
If you are casual, you are, or you pretend to be, relaxed and not very concerned about what is happening or what you are doing.

block[복습]
[blak]

v. (지나가지 못하게) 막다, 차단하다; **n.** 사각형 덩어리; 구역, 블록
If you block someone's way, you prevent them from going somewhere or entering a place by standing in front of them.

boot[*]
[bu:t]

v. 세게 차다; **n.** 목이 긴 신발, 부츠; 세게 차기
If you boot something such as a ball, you kick it hard.

all the way[복습]

idiom 완전히; 내내
You can use all the way to emphasize that your remark applies to every part of a situation, activity, or period of time.

smug
[smʌg]

a. 잘난 체하는, 점잖은 체하는
If you say that someone is smug, you are criticizing the fact they seem very pleased with how good, clever, or lucky they are.

bounce[복습]
[bauns]

v. 튀다, 튀게 하다; 급히 움직이다, 뛰어다니다; **n.** 튐, 바운드
If something bounces off a surface or is bounced off it, it reaches the surface and is reflected back.

charge[**]
[tʃa:rdʒ]

v. 돌격하다, 돌진하다; 청구하다; 충전하다, 채우다; **n.** 요금; 책임
If you charge toward someone or something, you move quickly and aggressively toward them.

dribble
[dribl]

v. (공을) 드리블하다; (액체가 조금씩) 똑똑 떨어지다; n. 조금씩 흘러내리는 것
When players dribble the ball in a game such as football or basketball, they keep kicking or tapping it quickly in order to keep it moving.

collide*
[kəláid]

v. 충돌하다, 부딪치다; (의지·목적 등이) 일치하지 않다, 상충하다
If two or more moving people or objects collide, they crash into one another.

harmless*
[háːrmlis]

a. 해롭지 않은, 무해한 (harmlessly ad. 해롭지 않게, 피해가 없게)
If you describe someone or something as harmless, you mean that they are not important and therefore unlikely to annoy other people or cause trouble.

heel**
[hiːl]

n. 뒤꿈치; (동물의) 발; 뒤축
Your heel is the back part of your foot, just below your ankle.

foul*
[faul]

n. 파울, 반칙; v. 반칙을 범하다; a. (냄새가) 더러운, 악취 나는
A foul is an act in a game or sport that is not allowed according to the rules.

tap*
[tæp]

v. (가볍게) 톡톡 두드리다; n. 수도꼭지; (가볍게) 두드리기
If you tap something, you hit it with a quick light blow or a series of quick light blows.

knock복습
[nak]

v. 치다, 부수다; (문을) 두드리다, 노크하다
If you knock something, you touch or hit it roughly, especially so that it falls or moves.

defend*
[difénd]

v. 방어하다, 수비하다
If you defend someone or something, you take action in order to protect them.

soar*
[sɔːr]

v. (허공으로) 솟구치다; (가치·물가 등이) 급등하다
If something such as a bird soars into the air, it goes quickly up into the air.

trace*
[treis]

n. 자취, 흔적; 극미량, 조금; v. 추적하다, (추적하여) 찾아내다
A trace is a sign which shows you that someone or something has been in a place.

scornful*
[skɔ́ːrnfəl]

a. 경멸하는, 멸시하는 (scornfully ad. 경멸적으로, 깔보고)
If you are scornful of someone or something, you show contempt for them.

chase**
[tʃeis]

v. 뒤쫓다; 추구하다; 쫓아내다; n. 추적, 추격
If you chase someone, or chase after them, you run after them or follow them quickly in order to catch or reach them.

obvious복습
[ábviəs]

a. 명백한, 분명한 (obviously ad. 분명히, 명백하게)
If something is obvious, it is easy to see or understand.

jog*
[dʒag]

v. 천천히 달리다, 조깅하다; n. 조깅
If you jog, you run slowly, often as a form of exercise.

freckle복습
[frekl]

n. 주근깨
Freckles are small light brown spots on someone's skin, especially on their face.

drip[*]
[drip]

v. 방울방울 떨어지다; 넘칠 듯이 지니고 있다
When liquid drips somewhere, or you drip it somewhere, it falls in individual small drops.

exhale
[ekshéil]

v. (숨 · 연기 등을) 내쉬다, 내뿜다
When you exhale, you breathe out the air that is in your lungs.

elated
[iléitid]

a. 마냥 행복해하는, 신이 난
If you are elated, you are extremely happy and excited because of something that has happened.

1분에 몇 단어를 읽는지 리딩 속도를 측정해보세요.

$$\frac{1,213 \text{ words}}{\text{reading time } (\quad) \text{ sec}} \times 60 = (\quad) \text{ WPM}$$

Build Your Vocabulary

pang^{복습}
[pæŋ]

n. 비통, 상심; 격통, 고통
A pang is a sudden strong feeling or emotion, for example of sadness or pain.

remorse
[rimɔ́ːrs]

n. 회한
Remorse is a strong feeling of sadness and regret about something wrong that you have done.

stuff^{복습}
[stʌf]

v. 채워 넣다, 속을 채우다; **n.** 것(들), 물건, 물질
If you stuff something somewhere, you push it there quickly and roughly.

greet^{복습}
[griːt]

v. 맞다, 환영하다
When you greet someone, you say 'Hello' or shake hands with them.

strike***
[straik]

v. (struck–stricken/struck) 갑자기 떠오르다; 치다, 부딪치다; 발생하다, 덮치다; **n.** 파업; 공격, 공습
If an idea or thought strikes you, it suddenly comes into your mind.

tardy*
[táːrdi]

a. 느린, 더딘; (도착 등이) 늦은, 지체된
If you describe something or someone as tardy, you think that they are later than they should be or later than expected.

whisper^{복습}
[hwíspəːr]

v. 속삭이다
When you whisper, you say something very quietly.

wiggle
[wigl]

v. (좌우 · 상하로 짧게) 씰룩씰룩[꼼지락꼼지락] 움직이다
If you wiggle something or if it wiggles, it moves up and down or from side to side in small quick movements.

gesture**
[dʒéstʃər]

v. (손 · 머리 · 얼굴 등으로) 가리키다, 몸짓을 하다; **n.** 몸짓
If you gesture, you use movements of your hands or head in order to tell someone something or draw their attention to something.

snicker^{복습}
[sníkər]

v. 낄낄 웃다, 숨죽여 웃다; **n.** 낄낄 웃음
If you snicker, you laugh quietly in a disrespectful way, for example at something rude or embarrassing.

approach^{복습}
[əpróutʃ]

v. 접근하다, 다가오다 **n.** 접근, 가까움
When you approach something, you get closer to it.

oblige*
[əbláidʒ]

v. 의무적으로 ~하게 하다; 돕다, (도움 등을) 베풀다
If you are obliged to do something, a situation, rule, or law makes it necessary for you to do that thing.

struggle[**]
[strʌgl]

v. 투쟁하다, 몸부림치다, 허우적거리다; **n.** 투쟁, 분투
If you struggle to do something, you try hard to do it, even though other people or things may be making it difficult for you to succeed.

bracelet[*]
[bréislit]

n. 팔찌
A bracelet is a chain or band, usually made of metal, which you wear around your wrist as jewelry.

jingle[*]
[dʒiŋgl]

v. 짤랑짤랑 소리를 내다; **n.** 딸랑딸랑 울리는 소리
When something jingles or when you jingle it, it makes a gentle ringing noise, like small bells.

light up[복습]

idiom (기쁘거나 신이 나서 두 눈·얼굴이) 환해지다
If your eyes light up, you suddenly look very surprised or happy.

exclaim[복습]
[ikskléim]

v. 외치다, 소리치다
If you exclaim, you say or shout something suddenly because of surprise, fear and pleasure.

inconspicuous
[inkənspíkjuəs]

a. 이목을 끌지 못하는, 눈에 잘 안 띄는
(inconspicuously **ad.** 눈에 띄지 않아, 주의를 끌지 않아)
Something that is inconspicuous is not easily seen or does not attract attention because it is small, ordinary, or hidden away.

fly[***]
[flai]

n. (바지 앞의) 지퍼로 잠그는 부분; 파리; **v.** (새·곤충이) 날다
The front opening on a pair of trousers is referred to as the fly. It usually consists of a zip or row of buttons behind a band of cloth.

hysterical
[histérikəl]

a. 히스테리 상태의, 발작적인
Hysterical laughter is loud and uncontrolled.

big deal[복습]
[bíg dí:l]

int. 그게 무슨 대수라고!; **n.** 대단한 것, 큰 일
(no big deal **int.** 별일 아니다, 대수롭지 않다)
You can say 'big deal' to someone to show that you are not impressed by something that they consider important or impressive.

draw[***]
[drɔ:]

v. (사람의 마음을) 끌다; (연필·펜·분필 등으로) 그리다; **n.** 추첨, 제비 뽑기
If you draw someone's attention to something, you make them aware of it or make them think about it.

tap[복습]
[tæp]

v. (가볍게) 톡톡 두드리다; **n.** 수도꼭지; (가볍게) 두드리기
If you tap something, you hit it with a quick light blow or a series of quick light blows.

pervert[복습]
[pərvə́:rt]

n. 변태, 성도착자
If you say that someone is a pervert, you mean that you consider their behavior, especially their sexual behavior, to be immoral or unacceptable.

bunch[*]
[bʌnʧ]

n. (양·수가) 많음; 다발, 묶음; **v.** 단단해지다, 단단하게 만들다
A bunch of things is a number of things, especially a large number.

naked[*]
[néikid]

a. (몸의 일부가) 드러난, 벌거벗은; 적나라한
Someone who is naked is not wearing any clothes.

count ^{복습}
[kaunt]

v. (정식으로) 인정되다; 수를 세다, 계산하다; 중요하다; n. 셈, 계산
If something counts or is counted as a particular thing, it is regarded as being that thing, especially in particular circumstances or under particular rules.

shrug ^{복습}
[ʃrʌg]

v. (양 손바닥을 내보이면서 어깨를) 으쓱하다; n. (어깨를) 으쓱하기
If you shrug, you raise your shoulders to show that you are not interested in something or that you do not know or care about something.

pretend ^{복습}
[priténd]

v. ~인 체하다, 가장하다; a. 가짜의, 꾸민
If you pretend that something is the case, you act in a way that is intended to make people believe that it is the case, although in fact it is not.

scenery [*]
[síːnəri]

n. 풍경; 배경, 무대 장치
The scenery in a country area is the land, water, or plants that you can see around you.

underpants ^{복습}
[ʌ́ndərpænts]

n. 팬티
Underpants are a piece of underwear which have two holes to put your legs through and elastic around the top to hold them up round your waist or hips.

witchcraft
[wítʃkræft]

n. 사악한 목적의 마법, 마술
Witchcraft is the use of magic powers, especially evil ones

logical [*]
[ládʒikəl]

a. 타당한, 사리에 맞는; 논리적인
Something that is logical seems reasonable or sensible in the circumstances.

scientific ^{**}
[sàiəntífik]

a. 과학적인
Scientific is used to describe things that relate to science or to a particular science

explanation [*]
[èksplənéiʃən]

n. 해명, 이유; 설명
If you say there is an explanation for something, you mean that there is a reason for it.

astrology
[əstrálədʒi]

n. 점성술, 점성학
Astrology is the study of the movements of the planets, sun, moon, and stars in the belief that these movements can have an influence on people's lives.

fortune ^{**}
[fɔ́ːrtʃən]

n. 운, 행운; 부, 재산
When someone tells your fortune, they tell you what they think will happen to you in the future, which they say is shown, for example, by the lines on your hand.

coincidence
[kouínsidəns]

n. (우연의) 일치, 부합; 동시에 일어남
A coincidence is when two or more similar or related events occur at the same time by chance and without any planning.

bind ^{**}
[baind]

v. (bound-bound) (약속 등으로) 의무를 지우다, 구속하다; 묶다
If you are bound by something such as a rule, agreement, or restriction, you are forced or required to act in a certain way.

now and then

idiom 때때로, 가끔
If you say that something happens now and then, you mean that it happens sometimes but not very often or regularly.

charge ^{복습}
[ʧaːrdʒ]

n. 책임; 요금; v. 돌격하다, 돌진하다; 청구하다; 충전하다, 채우다
If you are in charge in a particular situation, you are the most senior person and have control over something or someone.

curse ^{복습}
[kəːrs]

n. 저주; 욕(설), 악담; v. 욕(설)을 하다; 저주를 내리다
If you say that there is a curse on someone, you mean that there seems to be a supernatural power causing unpleasant things to happen to them.

lightning *
[láitniŋ]

n. 번개, 번갯불; a. 번개의, 번개 같은; 매우 빠른 (lightning bolt n. 번개불)
Lightning is the very bright flashes of light in the sky that happen during thunderstorms.

pitcher ^{복습}
[pítʃər]

① n. 물 주전자 ② n. 투수, 피처
A pitcher is a jug.

sidewalk *
[sáidwɔːk]

n. (포장한) 보도, 인도
A sidewalk is a path with a hard surface by the side of a road.

footprint
[fútprìnt]

n. 발자국
A footprint is a mark in the shape of a foot that a person or animal makes in or on a surface.

1분에 몇 단어를 읽는지 리딩 속도를 측정해보세요.

$$\frac{141 \text{ words}}{\text{reading time (} \quad \text{) sec}} \times 60 = (\quad) \text{ WPM}$$

Build Your Vocabulary

ghostly
[góustli]

a. 유령 같은; 유령이 많은
Something that is ghostly seems unreal or unnatural and may be frightening because of this.

counterpart
[káuntərpà:rt]

n. 상대, 대응 관계에 있는 것
Someone's or something's counterpart is another person or thing that has a similar function or position in a different place.

definition*
[dèfəníʃən]

n. (사전에 나오는 단어나 구의) 정의
A definition is a statement giving the meaning of a word or expression, especially in a dictionary.

collegiate
[kəlí:dʒtət]

a. 대학(생)의
Collegiate means belonging or relating to a college or to college students.

regurgitate 복습
[rigə:rdʒətèit]

v. (삼킨 음식물을 입 안으로 다시) 역류시키다; (듣거나 읽은 내용을 별 생각 없이) 반복하다
If a person or animal regurgitates food, they bring it back up from their stomach before it has been digested.

throw up

idiom ~을 토하다, 게우다
When someone throws up, they bring food they have eaten back out of mouth.

recall*
[rikɔ́:l]

v. 기억해 내다, 상기하다
When you recall something, you remember it and tell others about it.

puke
[pju:k]

v. 토하다
When someone pukes, they vomit

flip off 복습

idiom 손가락으로 욕을 하다
If you flip someone off, you raise your middle finger to them in a very rude sign.

fly 복습
[flai]

n. (바지 앞의) 지퍼로 잠그는 부분; 파리; **v.** (새 · 곤충이) 날다
The front opening on a pair of trousers is referred to as the fly. It usually consists of a zip or row of buttons behind a band of cloth.

1분에 몇 단어를 읽는지 리딩 속도를 측정해보세요.

$$\frac{662 \text{ words}}{\text{reading time } (\quad) \text{ sec}} \times 60 = (\qquad) \text{ WPM}$$

Build Your Vocabulary

attention [복습]
[əténʃən]

n. 주의 (집중), 주목
If you give someone or something your attention, you look at it, listen to it, or think about it carefully.

smirk
[smə:rk]

v. 능글맞게 웃다
If you smirk, you smile in an unpleasant way, often because you believe that you have gained an advantage over someone else or know something that they do not know.

instant[*]
[ínstənt]

a. 즉시의, 즉각적인; **n.** 즉시, 순간 (instantly **ad.** 즉시, 순간에)
You use instant to describe something that happens immediately.

straighten[*]
[stréitn]

v. 똑바르게 하다, 곧게 하다
If you straighten something, you make it tidy or put it in its proper position.

anxious[***]
[ǽŋkʃəs]

a. 걱정하는, 염려하는; 열망하는, 간절히 바라는 (anxiously **ad.** 걱정스럽게)
If you are anxious to do something or anxious that something should happen, you very much want to do it or very much want it to happen.

nerve[**]
[nə:rv]

n. (어려움 · 위험에 맞서는) 용기, 대담성; 신경; **v.** 용기를 내어 ~하다
Nerve is the courage that you need in order to do something difficult or dangerous.

drug[**]
[drʌg]

n. (불법적인) 약물, 마약; 의약품, 약
Drugs are substances that some people take because of their pleasant effects, but which are usually illegal.

comb[*]
[koum]

v. 빗다, 빗질하다; **n.** 빗(질)
When you comb your hair, you tidy it using a flat piece of plastic or metal with narrow pointed teeth along one side.

glance [복습]
[glæns]

v. 흘긋 보다, 잠깐 보다; **n.** 흘긋 봄
If you glance at something or someone, you look at them very quickly and then look away again immediately.

definite [복습]
[défənit]

a. 확실한, 확고한; 분명한, 뚜렷한 (definitely **ad.** 확실히, 명확히)
If something such as a decision or an arrangement is definite, it is firm and clear, and unlikely to be changed.

automobile[*]
[ɔ́:təməbí:l]

n. 자동차
An automobile is a car.

naked^{복습}
[néikid]

a. (몸의 일부가) 드러난, 벌거벗은; 적나라한
Someone who is naked is not wearing any clothes.

broken-down
[bróukən-daun]

a. 완전히 망가진
A broken-down vehicle or machine no longer works because it has something wrong with it.

disgust[*]
[disgʌ́st]

v. 혐오감을 유발하다, 역겹게 만들다; **n.** 혐오감, 역겨움, 넌더리
To disgust someone means to make them feel a strong sense of dislike and disapproval.

afford^{**}
[əfɔ́:rd]

v. (~을 살 · 할 · 금전적 · 시간적) 여유가 되다, 형편이 되다
If you cannot afford something, you do not have enough money to pay for it.

kick^{***}
[kik]

n. (강한) 쾌감, 스릴; 차기, 발길질; **v.** (발로) 차다
If something gives you a kick, it makes you feel very excited or very happy for a short period of time.

stringy
[stríɲi]

a. (머리카락이 길고 감지 않은 것처럼) 지저분한; (씹기 어렵게) 섬유질이 많은
Stringy hair is long, thin, and dirty.

nod^{복습}
[nad]

v. (고개를) 끄덕이다; **n.** (고개를) 끄덕임
If you nod, you move your head downward and upward to show agreement, understanding, or approval.

stare^{복습}
[stɛər]

v. 빤히 쳐다보다, 응시하다; **n.** 빤히 쳐다보기, 응시
If you stare at someone or something, you look at them for a long time.

hardly^{복습}
[há:rdli]

ad. 거의 ~아니다, 전혀 ~않다
When you say you can hardly do something, you are emphasizing that it is very difficult for you to do it.

poverty[*]
[pávərti]

n. 가난, 빈곤
Poverty is the state of being extremely poor.

petty
[péti]

a. 사소한, 하찮은; 옹졸한, 쩨쩨한
You can use petty to describe things such as problems, rules, or arguments which you think are unimportant or relate to unimportant things.

insignificant[*]
[insigní fikənt]

a. 대수롭지 않은, 사소한, 하찮은
Something that is insignificant is unimportant, especially because it is very small.

so-called^{복습}
[sóu-kɔ:ld]

a. 소위, 이른바; 흔히 ~라고 일컬어지는
You use so-called to indicate that you think a word or expression used to describe someone or something is in fact wrong.

stack[*]
[stæk]

n. 무더기, 더미; **v.** 쌓다, 포개다
A stack of things is a pile of them.

abrupt^{복습}
[əbrʌ́pt]

a. 갑작스러운, 뜻밖의; 퉁명스러운 (abruptly **ad.** 갑자기)
An abrupt change or action is very sudden, often in a way which is unpleasant.

trash ^{복습}
[træʃ]

n. 쓰레기; **v.** 부수다, 엉망으로 만들다
Trash consists of unwanted things or waste material such as used paper, empty containers and bottles, and waste food.

bin
[bin]

n. 쓰레기통; (뚜껑이 달린 저장용) 통
A bin is a container that you put rubbish in.

1. Why did David think that it was easier for Mo to stand up
   to Randy and Alvin?
   A. He thought that Mo liked to fight.
   B. He thought that Mo was bigger than him.
   C. He thought that Mo already beat up Randy.
   D. He thought that they wouldn't fight a girl.

2. Which of the following was NOT true about Mo?
   A. She took back David's project from Randy.
   B. She owned a big dog named Killer.
   C. She was building a dog house in shop class.
   D. She thought David's project was a heart at first but then saw an
      apple.

3. Why was science David's favorite subject?
   A. Science made sense.
   B. His father was a scientist.
   C. Science sometimes gave different results.
   D. He turned into a mad scientist in class.

4. What did David think would happen if Roger had dropped
   the beaker instead?
   A. David would become more popular.
   B. Roger would be teased by his friends.
   C. Roger would be seen as cool.
   D. Everyone else would break breakers on purpose.

5. Which of the following is NOT how Larry thought about
   Mo?
   A. He thought she was funny.
   B. He thought she was pretty.
   C. He thought she should grow her hair out.
   D. He thought she looked like girls in France.

6. What was David certain that he wouldn't do?
   A. He was certain that he wouldn't break the curse.
   B. He was certain that he wouldn't make friends.
   C. He was certain that he wouldn't apologize to Mrs. Bayfield.
   D. He was certain that he wouldn't pour lemonade on his face.

7. How did David offer to help Mo with her doghouse?
   A. He offered to help carry it with Larry.
   B. He offered to help make a new sign for her.
   C. He offered to help Mo get her dog to like it.
   D. He offered to take it to his house for his own dog.

1분에 몇 단어를 읽는지 리딩 속도를 측정해보세요.

$$\frac{636 \text{ words}}{\text{reading time (\quad) sec}} \times 60 = (\qquad) \text{ WPM}$$

Build Your Vocabulary

rub[**]
[rʌb]

v. 비비다, 문지르다; 스치다; **n.** 문지르기
If you rub a part of your body, you move your hand or fingers backwards and forwards over it while pressing firmly.

sandpaper
[sǽndpèipər]

n. 사포
Sandpaper is strong paper that has a coating of sand on it. It is used for rubbing wood or metal surfaces to make them smoother.

nameplate
[néimplèit]

n. 명찰, 문패
A piece of metal or plastic fastened onto something to show who owns it, who has made it, or who lives or works there.

entrance[**]
[éntrəns]

n. (출)입구, 문; 입장, 등장
The entrance to a place is the way into it, for example a door or gate.

thumb[**]
[θʌm]

n. 엄지손가락; **v.** (책을) 엄지손가락으로 넘기다
Your thumb is the short thick part on the side of your hand next to your four fingers.

bang[복습]
[bæŋ]

v. 쾅[탕] 하고 치다; 쾅 하고 닫다; **n.** 쾅[쿵] (하는 소리)
If you bang on something or if you bang it, you hit it hard, making a loud noise.

shrug[복습]
[ʃrʌg]

v. (양 손바닥을 내보이면서 어깨를) 으쓱하다; **n.** (어깨를) 으쓱하기
If you shrug, you raise your shoulders to show that you are not interested in something or that you do not know or care about something.

sand[**]
[sænd]

v. (매끈해지도록) 사포로 닦다; **n.** 모래
If you sand a wood or metal surface, you rub sandpaper over it in order to make it smooth or clean.

lean[복습]
[liːn]

v. ~에 기대다; 기울이다, (몸을) 숙이다
If you lean on or against someone or something, you rest against them so that they partly support your weight.

flat[***]
[flæt]

a. 생기가 없는; 평평한, 편평한 (flatly **ad.** 심드렁하게)
You use flat to describe someone's voice when they are saying something without expressing any emotion.

hang around (with someone)[복습]

idiom ~와 많이 어울리다
If you hang around with someone, you spend a lot of time with them.

mutter ^{복습} [mʌ́tər]	**v.** 중얼거리다; 투덜거리다; **n.** 중얼거림 If you mutter, you speak very quietly so that you cannot easily be heard, often because you are complaining about something.
recess ^{복습} [risés]	**n.** (학교의) 쉬는 시간; 휴회 A recess is a short period of time when you have a rest or a change from what you are doing, especially if you are working or if you are in a boring or unpleasant situation.
curly ^{복습} [kə́:rli]	**a.** 곱슬곱슬한 Curly hair is full of curls.
go for	**idiom** ~을 좋아하다, 선호하다; ~에 해당되다 If you go for someone or something, you prefer or like them.
grab ^{복습} [græb]	**v.** 붙잡다, 움켜잡다; **n.** 움켜잡으려고 함 If you grab something, you take it or pick it up suddenly and roughly.
protect ^{**} [prətékt]	**v.** 보호하다, 막다, 지키다 To protect someone or something means to prevent them from being harmed or damaged.
stand up to	**idiom** (용감히) 맞서다 If you stand up to someone or something, you resist them or defend your position against them.
push someone around	**idiom** ~에게 마구 이래라저래라 하다 If you push someone around, you order them to do things in a threatening or unpleasant way.
stem ^{복습} [stem]	**n.** 줄기, 대 The stem of a plant is the thin, upright part on which the flowers and leaves grow.
nail ^{복습} [neil]	**v.** 못으로 박다, 고정하다; **n.** 못; 손톱; 발톱 If you nail something somewhere, you fix it there using thin piece of metal with one pointed end and one flat end.

1분에 몇 단어를 읽는지 리딩 속도를 측정해보세요.

$$\frac{1{,}670 \text{ words}}{\text{reading time (\quad) sec}} \times 60 = (\quad) \text{ WPM}$$

Build Your Vocabulary

make sense

idiom 의미가 통하다, 말이 되다
If something makes sense, it has a meaning that you can easily understand.

logical 복습
[ládʒikəl]

a. 타당한, 사리에 맞는; 논리적인 (logically **ad.** 논리적으로)
Something that is logical seems reasonable or sensible in the circumstances.

consistent*
[kənsístənt]

a. 일관된
Someone who is consistent always behaves in the same way, has the same attitudes towards people or things.

gravity**
[grǽvəti]

v. (지구) 중력
Gravity is the force which causes things to drop to the ground.

hydrogen*
[háidrədʒən]

n. 수소
Hydrogen is a colorless gas that is the lightest and commonest element in the universe.

oxygen**
[áksidʒen]

n. 산소
Oxygen is a colorless gas that exists in large quantities in the air. All plants and animals need oxygen in order to live.

assist***
[əsíst]

v. 돕다; (어떤 일에) 도움이 되다; **n.** (스포츠에서) 어시스트
If you assist someone, you help them to do a job or task by doing part of the work for them.

experiment 복습
[ikspérəmənt]

n. (과학적인) 실험
An experiment is a scientific test which is done in order to discover what happens to something in particular conditions.

chemical*
[kémikəl]

n. 화학 물질; **a.** 화학의
Chemicals are substances that are used in a chemical process or made by a chemical process.

instant 복습
[ínstənt]

a. 즉시의, 즉각적인; **n.** 즉시, 순간 (instantly **ad.** 즉시, 순간에)
You use instant to describe something that happens immediately.

whisper 복습
[hwíspər]

v. 속삭이다
When you whisper, you say something very quietly.

fly 복습
[flai]

n. (바지 앞의) 지퍼로 잠그는 부분; 파리; **v.** (새 · 곤충이) 날다
The front opening on a pair of trousers is referred to as the fly. It usually consists of a zip or row of buttons behind a band of cloth.

pervert ^{복습}
[pərvə́:rt]

n. 변태, 성도착자
If you say that someone is a pervert, you mean that you consider their behavior, especially their sexual behavior, to be immoral or unacceptable.

pick on

idiom (부당하게) ~을 괴롭히다; ~을 선택하다
If you pick on someone, you treat them badly or unfairly, especially repeatedly.

foul ^{복습}
[faul]

a. (냄새가) 더러운, 악취 나는; **v.** 반칙을 범하다; **n.** 파울, 반칙
If you describe something as foul, you mean it is dirty and smells or tastes unpleasant.

snicker ^{복습}
[sníkər]

v. 낄낄 웃다, 숨죽여 웃다; **n.** 낄낄 웃음
If you snicker, you laugh quietly in a disrespectful way, for example at something rude or embarrassing.

laughter *
[lǽftə:r]

n. 웃음, 웃음소리
Laughter is the sound of people laughing, for example because they are amused or happy.

rotten *
[ratn]

a. 썩은, 부패한; 형편없는, 끔찍한
If food, wood, or another substance is rotten, it has decayed and can no longer be used.

depress *
[diprés]

v. 우울하게 하다, 낙담시키다 (depressed **a.** 우울한)
If someone or something depresses you, they make you feel sad and disappointed.

trivial *
[tríviəl]

a. 하찮은, 사소한; **n.** 하찮은 일
If you describe something as trivial, you think that it is unimportant and not serious.

compare **
[kəmpéər]

v. 비교하다, 대조하다; 비유하다
When you compare things, you consider them and discover the differences or similarities between them.

laugh one's head off

idiom 자지러지게 웃다, (남의 일에) 몹시 웃어대다
Phrase such as laugh your head off can be used to emphasize that someone is laughing or screaming a lot or very loudly.

slip ^{복습}
[slip]

v. (어떤 위치 · 손을 벗어나) 미끄러지다, 빠져 나가다; (재빨리 · 슬며시) 놓다; **n.** (작은 종이) 조각, 쪽지
If something slips, it slides out of place or out of your hand.

crash ^{복습}
[kræʃ]

v. 충돌하다, 부딪치다; **n.** (무엇이 떨어지거나 부서질 때 나는) 요란한 소리, 굉음
If something crashes somewhere, it moves and hits something else violently, making a loud noise.

explode *
[iksplóud]

v. 폭발하다, 격발하다; 폭발시키다
If someone explodes, they express strong feelings suddenly and violently.

tear ^{복습}
[tiər]

① **n.** 눈물 ② **v.** (tore—torn) 찢다, 찢어지다; **n.** 찢음
Tears are the drops of salty liquid that come out of your eyes when you are crying.

gag ^{복습}
[gæg]

① v. 말문을 막다, 재갈을 물리다; n. 재갈 ② n. 익살, 개그; v. 농담하다
If someone gags you, they tie a piece of cloth around your mouth in order to stop you from speaking or shouting.

cough**
[kɔːf]

v. 기침하다; n. (헛)기침
When you cough, you force air out of your throat with a sudden, harsh noise.

blacktop
[blǽktàip]

n. (포장에 쓰이는) 아스팔트 (도로)
Blacktop is a hard black substance which is used as a surface for roads.

take place

idiom (미리 준비되거나 계획된 일이) 일어나다
When something takes place, it happens, especially in a controlled or organized way.

molecule ^{복습}
[mάləkjùːl]

n. 분자
A molecule is the smallest amount of a chemical substance which can exist by itself.

disperse
[dispə́ːrs]

v. 퍼뜨리다, 흩뜨리다, 흩어지게 하다; a. 분산한
When something disperses or when you disperse it, it spreads over a wide area.

result***
[rizʌ́lt]

v. (~의 결과로) 발생하다; (어떤 원인에 의해 생긴) 결과, 결실
(resulting a. 결과로 초래된)
If something results in a particular situation or event, it causes that situation or event to happen.

odor*
[óudər]

n. (불쾌한) 냄새, 악취
An odor is a particular and distinctive smell.

scientific ^{복습}
[sàiəntífik]

a. 과학적인 (scientifically ad. 과학적 원리에 따라)
Scientific is used to describe things that relate to science or to a particular science.

pitcher ^{복습}
[pítʃər]

① n. 물 주전자 ② n. 투수, 피처
A pitcher is a jug.

brag
[bræg]

v. 자랑하다, 자만하다, 허풍떨다
If you brag, you say in a very proud way that you have something or have done something.

stink
[stiŋk]

v. (고약한) 냄새가 나다, 악취가 풍기다; n. 악취
To stink means to smell extremely unpleasant.

bomb**
[bam]

n. 폭탄; v. 폭탄으로 공격하다, 폭격하다
A bomb is a device which explodes and damages or destroys a large area.

puke ^{복습}
[pjuːk]

v. 토하다
When someone pukes, they vomit.

assure*
[əʃúər]

v. 안심시키다; 보증하다
If you assure someone that something is true or will happen, you tell them that it is definitely true or will definitely happen, often in order to make them less worried.

stuck
[stʌk]

a. ～을 떨쳐 버리지 못하는; 꽉 끼인, 움직일 수 없는
If you are stuck with something that you do not want, you cannot get rid of it.

bet*
[bet]

v. (～이) 틀림없다; (경마 · 내기 등에) 돈을 걸다; **n.** 내기; 내기 돈
You use expressions such as 'I bet,' 'I'll bet,' and 'you can bet' to indicate that you are sure something is true.

hopeful**
[hóupfəl]

a. 희망에 찬, 기대하는 (hopefully **ad.** 희망을 갖고)
If you are hopeful, you are fairly confident that something that you want to happen will happen.

concentrate**
[kánsəntrèit]

v. 집중하다, 집중시키다, 전념하다; **n.** 농축물
If you concentrate on something, you give all your attention to it.

swallow**
[swálou]

v. 삼키다, 목구멍으로 넘기다; (초조해서) 마른침을 삼키다
If you swallow something, you cause it to go from your mouth down into your stomach.

nerd복습
[nəːrd]

n. 멍청하고 따분한 사람
If you say that someone is a nerd, you mean that they are stupid or ridiculous, especially because they wear unfashionable clothes or show too much interest in computers or science.

naked복습
[néikid]

a. (몸의 일부가) 드러난, 벌거벗은; 적나라한
Someone who is naked is not wearing any clothes.

rescue*
[réskjuː]

v. (위험에서) 구하다, 구출하다; **n.** 구출, 구조, 구제
If you rescue someone, you get them out of a dangerous or unpleasant situation.

automatic**
[ɔ̀ːtəmǽtik]

a. (어떤 행동 · 상황에 대한 결과가) 자동적으로 따라오는; 자동의; 무의식적인 (automatically **ad.** 자동적으로)
If something such as an action or a punishment is automatic, it happens without people needing to think about it because it is the result of a fixed rule or method.

snot
[snat]

n. 버릇없는 사람; 콧물 (snotty **a.** 건방진)
If you call someone a snot, you mean they are rude and annoying.

weird복습
[wiərd]

a. 이상한, 기묘한; 수상한
If you describe something or someone as weird, you mean that they are strange.

strike복습
[straik]

v. (struck–stricken/struck) 갑자기 떠오르다; 치다, 부딪치다; 발생하다, 덮치다; **n.** 파업; 공격, 공습
If an idea or thought strikes you, it suddenly comes into your mind.

simultaneous*
[saiməltéiniəs]

a. 동시의, 동시에 일어나는 (simultaneously **ad.** 동시에)
Things which are simultaneous happen or exist at the same time.

proper복습
[prápər]

a. 적절한, 제대로 된
The proper thing is the one that is correct or most suitable.

formal***
[fɔ́ːrməl]

a. 격식을 차린, 정중한; 공식적인, 정식의
Formal speech or behavior is very correct and serious rather than relaxed and friendly, and is used especially in official situations.

obvious ^{복습}
[ábviəs]

a. 명백한, 분명한 (obviously **ad.** 분명히, 명백하게)
If something is obvious, it is easy to see or understand.

petite
[pətí:t]

a. 자그마한
If a woman or girl is petite, she is small and thin in an attractive way.

shade^{**}
[ʃeid]

n. (pl.) 선글라스; (시원한) 그늘; 색조; **v.** 그늘지게 하다
Shades are sunglasses.

cheek^{**}
[tʃi:k]

n. 뺨, 볼
Your cheeks are the sides of your face below your eyes.

redden
[redn]

v. 빨개지다, 붉어지다
If someone reddens or their face reddens, their face turns pink or red, often because they are embarrassed or angry.

stuff ^{복습}
[stʌf]

n. 것(들), 물건, 물질; **v.** 채워 넣다, 속을 채우다
You can use stuff to refer to things such as a substance, a collection of things, events, or ideas, or the contents of something in a general way without mentioning the thing itself by name.

sigh ^{복습}
[sai]

v. 한숨 쉬다; **n.** 한숨, 탄식
When you sigh, you let out a deep breath, as a way of expressing feelings such as disappointment, tiredness, or pleasure.

remind^{**}
[rimáind]

v. 생각나게 하다, 상기시키다, 일깨우다
If someone reminds you of a fact or event that you already know about, they say something which makes you think about it.

64

1분에 몇 단어를 읽는지 리딩 속도를 측정해보세요.

$$\frac{753 \text{ words}}{\text{reading time (\quad) sec}} \times 60 = (\qquad) \text{ WPM}$$

Build Your Vocabulary

crummy
[krʌ́mi]

a. 형편없는
Something that is crummy is unpleasant, of very poor quality, or not good enough.

pop ^{복습}
[pap]

v. 불쑥 나타나다; 펑[빵] 하는 소리가 나다; **n.** 펑[빵] (하고 터지는 소리)
If something pops, it moves quickly and suddenly, especially from a closed space.

rack *
[ræk]

n. 받침대, 선반
A rack is a frame or shelf, usually with bars or hooks, that is used for holding things or for hanging things on.

bend ^{복습}
[bend]

v. (bent–bent) 구부리다, 굽히다, 숙이다; **n.** 커브, 굽음, 굽은 곳
When you bend, you move the top part of your body downward and forward.

fiddle *
[fidl]

v. 만지작거리다; (구어) 바이올린을 켜다; **n.** 바이올린
To move things about or touch things with no particular purpose.

catch someone off guard

idiom ~의 방심을 틈타다, 허를 찌르다
If someone catches you off guard, they surprise you by doing something you do not expect.

befuddle
[bifʌ́dlmənt]

v. 어리둥절하게 하다; 정신을 잃게 하다 (befuddlement **n.** 어리둥절함)
If something befuddles you, it confuses your mind or thoughts.

hop *
[hap]

v. 깡충 뛰다, 뛰어오르다; **n.** 깡충깡충 뜀
If you hop, you move along by jumping.

fiasco
[fiǽskou]

n. 낭패
If you describe an event or attempt to do something as a fiasco, you are emphasizing that it fails completely.

stink ^{복습}
[stiŋk]

v. (고약한) 냄새가 나다, 악취가 풍기다; **n.** 악취
To stink means to smell extremely unpleasant.

delightful *
[diláitfəl]

a. 정말 기분 좋은
If you describe something or someone as delightful, you mean they are very pleasant.

tip ^{복습}
[tip]

v. 기울어지다, 젖히다; **n.** (뾰족한) 끝
If you tip an object or part of your body or if it tips, it moves into a sloping position with one end or side higher than the other.

amid
[əmíd]

prep. ~으로 에워싸인; (흥분 · 공포심이 느껴지는) 가운데에
If something is amid other things, it is surrounded by them.

formal^{복습}
[fɔ́:rməl]

a. 격식을 차린, 정중한; 공식적인, 정식의 (formally ad. 형식적으로)
Formal speech or behavior is very correct and serious rather than relaxed and friendly, and is used especially in official situations.

remind^{복습}
[rimáind]

v. 생각나게 하다, 상기시키다, 일깨우다
If someone reminds you of a fact or event that you already know about, they say something which makes you think about it.

risk***
[risk]

v. (~을) 위태롭게 하다, ~의 위험을 무릅쓰다; n. 위험
If you risk your life or something else important, you behave in a way that might result in it being lost or harmed.

wreck*
[rek]

v. 엉망으로 만들다, 결딴내다; 망가뜨리다, 파괴하다; n. 난파선
To wreck something means to completely destroy or ruin it.

daydream^{복습}
[déidrì:m]

v. 공상에 잠기다; n. 백일몽
If you daydream, you think about pleasant things for a period of time, usually about things that you would like to happen.

count^{복습}
[kaunt]

v. 수를 세다, 계산하다; 중요하다; (정식으로) 인정되다; n. 셈, 계산
When you count, you say all the numbers one after another up to a particular number.

freckle^{복습}
[frekl]

n. 주근깨
Freckles are small light brown spots on someone's skin, especially on their face.

desert**
[dizə́:rt]

① v. (어떤 장소를) 버리다, 떠나다 (deserted a. 사람이 없는) ② n. 사막, 황무지
If people or animals desert a place, they leave it and it becomes empty.

curse^{복습}
[kə:rs]

n. 저주; 욕(설), 악담; v. 욕(설)을 하다; 저주를 내리다
If you say that there is a curse on someone, you mean that there seems to be a supernatural power causing unpleasant things to happen to them.

serve***
[sə:rv]

v. (식당 등에서 음식을) 제공하다; (조직 · 국가 등을 위해) 일하다, 근무하다
When you serve food and drink, you give people food and drink.

refreshment*
[rifréʃmənt]

n. 다과, 가벼운 식사, 음료; 원기 회복, 상쾌하게 함
Refreshments are drinks and small amounts of food that are provided, for example, during a meeting or a journey.

triumphant
[traiʌ́mfənt]

a. 크게 성공한, 큰 승리를 거둔 (triumphantly ad. 의기양양하여)
Someone who is triumphant has gained a victory or succeeded in something and feels very happy about it.

exclaim^{복습}
[ikskléim]

v. 외치다, 소리치다
If you exclaim, you say or shout something suddenly because of surprise, fear and pleasure.

beat**
[bi:t]

v. (게임 · 시합에서) 이기다; 때리다, 두드리다; (심장이) 고동치다; n. 고동, 맥박
If you beat someone in a competition or election, you defeat them.

66

knowingly
[nóuiŋli]

ad. (사정 등을) 다 알고도, 고의로
If you knowingly do something wrong, you do it even though you know it is wrong.

assure ^{복습}
[əʃúər]

v. 안심시키다; 보증하다
If you assure someone that something is true or will happen, you tell them that it is definitely true or will definitely happen, often in order to make them less worried.

fair and square

idiom 공명정대하게, 정정당당하게
If you say that someone won a competition fair and square, you mean that they won honestly and without cheating.

knowingly
[nóuiŋli]

assure ^{복습}
[əʃúər]

1분에 몇 단어를 읽는지 리딩 속도를 측정해보세요.

$$\frac{1,588 \text{ words}}{\text{reading time (\quad) sec}} \times 60 = (\quad) \text{ WPM}$$

Build Your Vocabulary

lean ^{복습}
[li:n]

v. ~에 기대다; 기울이다. (몸을) 숙이다
If you lean on or against someone or something, you rest against them so that they partly support your weight.

depress ^{복습}
[diprés]

v. 우울하게 하다. 낙담시키다 (depressed **a. 우울한**)
If someone or something depresses you, they make you feel sad and disappointed.

glance ^{복습}
[glæns]

v. 흘긋 보다. 잠깐 보다; n. 흘긋 봄
If you glance at something or someone, you look at them very quickly and then look away again immediately.

entrance ^{복습}
[éntrəns]

n. (출)입구, 문; 입장, 등장
The entrance to a place is the way into it, for example a door or gate.

take it the wrong way

idiom (남의 말을 그의 의도와 달리) 기분 나쁘게 받아들이다
If you take it the wrong way, you fail to understand a statement or situation correctly and feel that someone is criticizing you when in fact they are not.

wimp
[wimp]

n. 겁쟁이, 약골
If you call someone a wimp, you disapprove of them because they lack confidence or determination, orbecause they are often afraid of things.

goofy
[gú:fi]

a. 바보 같은, 얼빠진
If you describe someone or something as goofy, you think they are rather silly or ridiculous.

intent*
[intént]

a. 강한 관심을 보이는, 몰두하는; n. 의도 (intently **ad. 골똘하게**)
If you are intent on doing something, you are eager and determined to do it.

distract*
[distrǽkt]

v. (마음 · 주의를) 흐트러뜨리다. 딴 데로 돌리다 (distracted **a. 마음이 산란해진**)
If something distracts you or your attention from something, it takes your attention away from it.

mood^{**}
[mu:d]

n. 기분; 분위기
Your mood is the way you are feeling at a particular time. If you are in a good mood, you feel cheerful. If you are in a bad mood, you feel angry and impatient.

bother ^{복습}
[báðər]

v. 귀찮게 하다. 귀찮게 말을 걸다; 신경 쓰다. 애를 쓰다; n. 성가심
If someone bothers you, they talk to you when you want to be left alone or interrupt you when you are busy.

delightful ^{복습}
[diláitfəl]

a. 정말 기분 좋은
If you describe something or someone as delightful, you mean they are very pleasant.

dumb ^{복습}
[dʌm]

a. (구어) 멍청한, 우둔한; 벙어리의, 말을 하지 않는
If you call a person dumb, you mean that they are stupid or foolish.

blues
[bluːz]

n. 우울; 블루스 (곡)
Blues is a feeling of depression or deep unhappiness.

puke ^{복습}
[pjuːk]

v. 토하다
When someone pukes, they vomit

stink ^{복습}
[stiŋk]

v. (고약한) 냄새가 나다, 악취가 풍기다; **n.** 악취
To stink means to smell extremely unpleasant.

ignore ^{복습}
[ignɔ́ːr]

v. 무시하다
If you ignore someone or something, you pay no attention to them.

lay off

idiom (명령형으로 쓰여) (~을) 그만둬
People say 'lay off' to tell someone to stop doing something that irritates or annoys them.

fart
[faːrt]

v. 방귀 뀌다; **n.** 방귀; 바보
If you fart, you emit digestive gases from your anus.

demand***
[dimǽnd]

v. 묻다, 요구하다, 청구하다; **n.** 요구, 수요
If you demand something such as information or action, you ask for it in a very forceful way.

stand up to ^{복습}

idiom (용감히) 맞서다
If you stand up to someone or something, you resist them or defend your position against them.

arrange**
[əréindʒ]

v. 준비하다; 가지런히 하다, 배열하다
If you arrange something, you make it possible to have or to do.

nod ^{복습}
[nad]

v. (고개를) 끄덕이다; **n.** (고개를) 끄덕임
If you nod, you move your head downward and upward to show agreement, understanding, or approval.

shade ^{복습}
[ʃeid]

n. (pl.) 선글라스; (시원한) 그늘; 색조; **v.** 그늘지게 하다
Shades are sunglasses.

tap ^{복습}
[tæp]

v. (가볍게) 톡톡 두드리다; **n.** 수도꼭지; (가볍게) 두드리기
If you tap something, you hit it with a quick light blow or a series of quick light blows.

entire*
[intáiər]

a. 전체의; 완전한
You use entire when you want to emphasize that you are referring to the whole of something, for example, the whole of a place, time, or population.

personality**
[pəːrsənǽliti]

n. 개성, 성격
Your personality is your whole character and nature.

period^{복습}
[píːəriəd]

n. (학교의 일과를 나눠 놓은) 시간; 기간, 시기; (여성의) 생리
At a school or college, a period is one of the parts that the day is divided into during which lessons or other activities take place.

big deal^{복습}
[bíg díːl]

int. 그게 무슨 대수라고!; n. 대단한 것, 큰 일
You can say 'big deal' to someone to show that you are not impressed by something that they consider important or impressive.

giggle[*]
[gigl]

v. 낄낄 웃다; n. 낄낄 웃음
If someone giggles, they laugh in a childlike way, because they are amused, nervous, or embarrassed.

abrupt^{복습}
[əbrʌ́pt]

a. 갑작스러운, 뜻밖의; 퉁명스러운 (abruptly ad. 갑자기)
An abrupt change or action is very sudden, often in a way which is unpleasant.

declare^{***}
[diklέər]

v. 선언하다; 단언하다
If you declare something, you state officially and formally that it exists or is the case.

figure^{복습}
[fígjər]

v. 생각하다, 판단하다; 계산하다; n. 모습, 인물; 숫자, 계산; 도형, 도표
If you figure that something is the case, you think or guess that it is the case.

grunt[*]
[grʌnt]

v. (사람이) 툴툴거리다; (돼지가) 꿀꿀거리다; n. 툴툴거리는 소리
If you grunt, you make a low sound, especially because you are annoyed or not interested in something.

rub^{복습}
[rʌb]

v. 비비다, 문지르다; 스치다; n. 문지르기
If you rub a part of your body, you move your hand or fingers backwards and forwards over it while pressing firmly.

doorway[*]
[dɔ́ːrwèi]

n. 출입구
A doorway is a space in a wall where a door opens and closes.

barely^{복습}
[bέərli]

ad. 간신히, 가까스로; 거의 ~않다
You use barely to say that something is only just true or only just the case.

bark[*]
[baːrk]

v. (개가) 짖다; n. 나무껍질; (개 등이) 짖는 소리
When a dog barks, it makes a short, loud noise, once or several times.

laughter^{복습}
[lǽftəːr]

n. 웃음, 웃음소리
Laughter is the sound of people laughing, for example because they are amused or happy.

warn^{복습}
[wɔːrn]

v. 경고하다, 주의를 주다, 조심하라고 하다
If you warn someone about something such as a possible danger or problem, you tell them about it so that they are aware of it.

bang^{복습}
[bæŋ]

v. 쾅[탕] 하고 치다; 쾅 하고 닫다; n. 쾅[쿵] (하는 소리)
If you bang on something or if you bang it, you hit it hard, making a loud noise.

chase^{복습}
[ʧeis]

v. 뒤쫓다; 추구하다; 쫓아내다; n. 추적, 추격
If you chase someone, or chase after them, you run after them or follow them quickly in order to catch or reach them.

yell ^{복습}
[jel]

v. 소리치다, 고함치다; **n.** 고함소리, 부르짖음
If you yell, you shout loudly, usually because you are excited, angry, or in pain.

elude
[ilúːd]

v. (교묘히) 피하다, 빠져나가다
If something that you want eludes you, you fail to obtain it.

trip ^{★★★}
[trip]

v. 걸려 넘어지다; 경쾌한 걸음걸이로 걷다; **n.** 여행
If you trip when you are walking, you knock your foot against something and fall or nearly fall.

remark ^{복습}
[rimáːrk]

n. (말이나 글로 의견·생각 등을 표하는) 발언, 언급; 발언하다
If you make a remark about something, you say something about it.

curly ^{복습}
[kə́ːrli]

a. 곱슬곱슬한
Curly hair is full of curls.

rotten ^{복습}
[ratn]

a. 형편없는, 끔찍한; 썩은, 부패한
If you describe something as rotten, you think it is very unpleasant or of very poor quality.

1. What did Mo offer David and Larry at her house?
    A. She offered them water in glasses with ice.
    B. She offered them glasses of lemonade.
    C. She offered them water from a hose.
    D. She offered them soda in cans.

2. Why had Mo built a doghouse?
    A. She used to have a dog named Killer.
    B. She wanted to sleep outside in it.
    C. She wanted people to think a dangerous dog lived there.
    D. She wanted to convince her parents to let her have a dog.

3. What did Mo say she noticed about Tori Williams?
    A. Mo noticed that Tori and David looked at each other.
    B. Mo noticed that Tori was dating Randy.
    C. Mo noticed that Tori stopped coming to school.
    D. Mo noticed that Tori was good at volleyball.

4. What did Tori offer to do for David at his locker?
    A. She offered to get the janitor to come help him.
    B. She offered to keep his books in her locker.
    C. She offered to do his homework for him.
    D. She offered to lend him her books.

5. How did David know that Scott and Ginger were a couple?

   A. Ginger was wearing Scott's jacket.

   B. Ginger and Scott were holding hands.

   C. He had heard a rumor from Larry.

   D. Scott told him that he liked Ginger.

6. Who did Ricky ask David about?

   A. Woody Allen

   B. Robin Williams

   C. The Three Musketeers

   D. The Three Stooges

7. Why did David tell Larry and Mo mean things about Mrs. Bayfield?

   A. He wanted to convince them that she was a witch.

   B. He wanted to scare them into avoiding her.

   C. He wanted to get revenge on Mrs. Bayfield by spreading rumors.

   D. He wanted them to ask Mrs. Bayfield to remove the curse for him.

1분에 몇 단어를 읽는지 리딩 속도를 측정해보세요.

$$\frac{983 \text{ words}}{\text{reading time (} \quad \text{) sec}} \times 60 = (\quad) \text{ WPM}$$

Build Your Vocabulary

heave[*]
[hi:v]

v. (한숨을) 쉬다; (무거운 것을) 들어 올리다, 내던지다; n. 들어 올리기
If you heave a sigh, you give a big sigh.

sigh[복습]
[sai]

n. 한숨, 탄식; v. 한숨 쉬다
If people breathe or heave a sigh of relief, they feel happy that something unpleasant has not happened or is no longer happening.

stretch[**]
[streʧ]

v. 기지개를 켜다; (팔 · 다리의 근육을) 당기다; 늘이다, 늘어지다; n. 기지개 켜기
When you stretch, you put your arms or legs out straight and tighten your muscles.

stiff[**]
[stif]

a. 단단한, 뻣뻣한; 완강한, 완고한
Something that is stiff is firm or does not bend easily.

cramp
[kræmp]

① v. 경련을 일으키다, 쥐가 나게 하다; n. (근육의) 경련 ② v. 막다, 방해하다
When you have cramped arms or legs, you suffer from sudden painful contraction of a muscle.

offer[***]
[ɔ́:fər]

v. 제안하다; 제공하다; n. 제공
If you offer something to someone, you ask them if they would like to have it or use it.

bush[복습]
[buʃ]

n. 관목, 덤불
A bush is a large plant which is smaller than a tree and has a lot of branches.

dart[*]
[da:rt]

v. (시선 · 화살 · 빛 등을) 던지다, 쏘다; n. 던지는 화살, 다트
If you dart a look at someone or something, or if your eyes dart to them, you look at them very quickly.

neat[복습]
[ni:t]

a. 뛰어난, 훌륭한; 정돈된, 단정한, 말쑥한
If you say that something is neat, you mean that it is very good.

logical[복습]
[ládʒikəl]

a. 타당한, 사리에 맞는; 논리적인
Something that is logical seems reasonable or sensible in the circumstances.

explanation[복습]
[èksplənéiʃən]

n. 해명, 이유; 설명
If you say there is an explanation for something, you mean that there is a reason for it.

make up for[복습]

idiom ~에 대해 보상하다, (잘못된 상황을 바로잡을 수 있도록) 만회하다
If you make up for something, you do something good for someone because you have treated them badly or because they have done something good for you.

insist[**]
[insíst]

v. 우기다, 주장하다; 강요하다
If you insist that something is the case, you say so very firmly and refuse to say otherwise, even though other people do not believe you.

pissant
[písænt]

n. 무가치한 사람
A pissant is an insignificant or contemptible person.

snap[*]
[snæp]

v. 딱[툭] (하고) 부러뜨리다; (화난 목소리로) 딱딱거리다; n. 찰칵 하는 소리
If you snap your fingers, you make a sharp sound by moving your middle finger quickly across your thumb, for example in order to accompany music or to order someone to do something.

blush[복습]
[blʌʃ]

v. 얼굴을 붉히다, 얼굴이 빨개지다; n. (당황하거나 수치스러워) 얼굴이 붉어짐
When you blush, your face becomes redder than usual because you are ashamed or embarrassed.

revolting
[rivóultiŋ]

a. 혐오스러운, 역겨운
If you say that something or someone is revolting, you mean you think they are horrible and disgusting.

blurt
[blə:rt]

v. 불쑥 말하다; 무심결에 누설하다
If someone blurts something, they say it suddenly, after trying hard to keep quiet or to keep it secret.

matter-of-fact
[mǽtər-əv-fǽkt]

a. 사무적인, 무미건조한; 사실의, 실제적인 (matter-of-factly **ad. 무미건조하게**)
If you describe a person as matter-of-fact, you mean that they show no emotions such as enthusiasm, anger, or surprise.

react[복습]
[riǽkt]

v. 반응하다, 반응을 보이다
When you react to something that has happened to you, you behave in a particular way because of it.

screw up

idiom 망치다, 엉망으로 만들다
To screw something up, or to screw up, means to cause something to fail or be spoiled.

impress[복습]
[imprés]

v. ~에게 (깊은) 인상을 주다; 감동시키다 (impression **n. 인상, 느낌**)
If something impresses you, you feel great admiration for it.

idiot[복습]
[ídiət]

n. 바보, 멍청이
If you call someone an idiot, you are showing that you think they are very stupid or have done something very stupid.

spill[*]
[spil]

v. 엎지르다, 흘리다; n. 엎지름, 유출
If a liquid spills or if you spill it, it accidentally flows over the edge of a container.

lap[복습]
[læp]

n. 무릎; (경주에서 트랙의) 한 바퀴
If you have something on your lap, it is on top of your legs and near to your body.

period[복습]
[pí:əriəd]

n. (여성의) 생리; 기간, 시기; (학교의 일과를 나눠 놓은) 시간
When a woman has a period, she bleeds from her womb. This usually happens once a month, unless she is pregnant.

embarrass ^{복습}
[imbǽrəs]

v. 당황스럽게 만들다 (embarrassed a. 쑥스러운, 어색한)
If something or someone embarrasses you, they make you feel shy or ashamed.

obvious ^{복습}
[ábviəs]

a. 명백한, 분명한 (obviously ad. 분명히, 명백하게)
If something is obvious, it is easy to see or understand.

1분에 몇 단어를 읽는지 리딩 속도를 측정해보세요.

$$\frac{1,194 \text{ words}}{\text{reading time (} \qquad \text{) sec}} \times 60 = (\qquad) \text{ WPM}$$

Build Your Vocabulary

miserable^{복습}
[mízərəbl]

a. 비참한, 우울한
If you describe the weather as miserable, you mean that it makes you feel depressed, because it is raining or dull.

mist^{**}
[mist]

n. 안개; **v.** 안개가 끼다, 눈이 흐려지다
Mist consists of a large number of tiny drops of water in the air, which make it difficult to see very far.

improve^{**}
[imprú:v]

v. 개선하다, 진보하다, 나아지다 (improvement **n.** 나아짐; 발전)
If something improves or if you improve it, it gets better.

flash^{복습}
[flæʃ]

v. (잠깐) 비치다, 번쩍이다; 비추다; (분노 등으로) 발끈[폭발]하다 **n.** 섬광, 번쩍임
If a light flashes or if you flash a light, it shines with a sudden bright light, especially as quick, regular flashes of light.

gallant
[gǽlənt]

a. 용감한; **n.** 멋진 청년 (gallantly **ad.** 용감하게; 씩씩하게)
If someone is gallant, they behave bravely and honorably in a dangerous or difficult situation.

distant^{**}
[dístənt]

a. 먼, (멀리) 떨어져 있는
Distant means very far away.

side by side

idiom 나란히
If two people or things are side by side, they are next to each other.

take a chance^{복습}

idiom 운에 맡기다, (모험치고) 해보다
When you take a chance, you try to do something although there is a large risk of danger or failure.

gloomy[*]
[glú:mi]

a. 어두운; 우울한
If a place is gloomy, it is almost dark so that you cannot see very well.

quirky
[kwə́:rki]

a. 꾀바른, 변덕스러운
Something or someone that is quirky is rather odd or unpredictable in their appearance, character, or behavior.

respective[*]
[rispéktiv]

a. 각각의, 저마다의, 각자의
Belonging to or relating to each person or thing you have just mentioned.

recess^{복습}
[risés]

n. (학교의) 쉬는 시간; 휴회
A recess is a short period of time when you have a rest or a change from what you are doing, especially if you are working or if you are in a boring or unpleasant situation.

relive
[rì:lív]

v. 다시 체험하다, 재현하다; 소생하다
If you relive something that has happened to you in the past, you remember it and imagine that you are experiencing it again.

redden ^{복습}
[redn]

v. 빨개지다, 붉어지다
If someone reddens or their face reddens, their face turns pink or red, often because they are embarrassed or angry.

glare *
[glɛər]

v. 노려보다; 번쩍번쩍 빛나다; n. 섬광; 노려봄
If you glare at someone, you look at them with an angry expression on your face.

turn the table

idiom 형세를 역전시키고 우위를 차지하다
If you turn the tables on someone, you change the situation completely, so that instead of them causing problems for you, you are causing problems for them.

occur ^{복습}
[əkə́:r]

v. 일어나다, 생기다; 생각이 떠오르다
When something occurs, it happens.

bet ^{복습}
[bet]

v. (~이) 틀림없다; (경마·내기 등에) 돈을 걸다; n. 내기; 내기 돈
You use expressions such as 'I bet', 'I'll bet', and 'you can bet' to indicate that you are sure something is true.

declare ^{복습}
[diklέər]

v. 선언하다; 단언하다 (declaration n. 선언; 단언)
If you declare something, you state officially and formally that it exists or is the case.

snot ^{복습}
[snat]

n. 버릇없는 사람; 콧물 (snotty a. 건방진)
If you call someone a snot, you mean they are rude and annoying.

spacey ^{복습}
[spéisi]

a. 멍한
You can use spacey to describe things, especially music, which seem strange, especially because they are very modern or like things in a dream.

wrap ^{복습}
[ræp]

v. 감싸다; 포장하다; n. 싸개, 덮개
If someone wraps their arms, fingers, or legs around something, they put them firmly around it.

press one's luck

idiom 과욕을 부려 일을 망치다
If you say that someone is pressing their luck, you think they are taking a bigger risk than is sensible, and may get into trouble.

combination ^{복습}
[kàmbənéiʃən]

n. (자물쇠 등을 열 수 있도록 숫자를 조합한 일련의) 번호; 결합, 화합, 조합
A combination is a sequence of numbers or letters used to open a lock.

sheepish ^{복습}
[ʃí:piʃ]

a. (어리석은·잘못된 짓을 하여) 멋쩍어 하는 (sheepishly ad. 수줍게, 어색하게)
If you look sheepish, you look slightly embarrassed because you feel foolish or you have done something silly.

shrug ^{복습}
[ʃrʌg]

v. (양 손바닥을 내보이면서 어깨를) 으쓱하다; n. (어깨를) 으쓱하기
If you shrug, you raise your shoulders to show that you are not interested in something or that you do not know or care about something.

curse ^{복습}
[kə:rs]

n. 저주; 욕(설), 악담; **v.** 욕(설)을 하다; 저주를 내리다
If you say that there is a curse on someone, you mean that there seems to be a supernatural power causing unpleasant things to happen to them.

mutter ^{복습}
[mʌ́tər]

v. 중얼거리다; 투덜거리다; **n.** 중얼거림
If you mutter, you speak very quietly so that you cannot easily be heard, often because you are complaining about something.

sink ***
[siŋk]

v. 가라앉다, 빠지다; **n.** (부엌의) 싱크대, 개수대 (sinking **a.** 가라앉는)
If you have a sinking feeling, you suddenly become depressed or lose hope.

pit *
[pit]

n. (크고 깊은) 구덩이
A pit is a large hole that is dug in the ground.

dare ^{복습}
[dɛər]

v. 감히 ~하다, 무릅쓰다, 도전하다
If you dare to do something, you do something which requires a lot of courage.

janitor
[dʒǽnitər]

n. 수위, 관리인
A janitor is a person whose job is to look after a building.

announce **
[ənáuns]

v. 발표하다, 알리다
If you announce something, you tell people about it publicly or officially.

trip ^{복습}
[trip]

v. 걸려 넘어지다; 경쾌한 걸음걸이로 걷다; **n.** 여행
If you trip when you are walking, you knock your foot against something and fall or nearly fall.

fringed
[frindʒd]

a. 술 장식이 달린
Fringed clothes, curtains, or lampshades are decorated with fringes.

leather **
[léðər]

n. 가죽
Leather is treated animal skin which is used for making shoes, clothes, bags, and furniture.

go steady

idiom (~와) 고정적으로 사귀다
If you go steady with someone, you have him or her as a regular boyfriend or girlfriend.

stare ^{복습}
[stɛər]

v. 빤히 쳐다보다, 응시하다; **n.** 빤히 쳐다보기, 응시
If you stare at someone or something, you look at them for a long time.

crack up ^{복습}

idiom 마구 웃기 시작하다
If you crack up, you suddenly start laughing a lot.

1분에 몇 단어를 읽는지 리딩 속도를 측정해보세요.

$$\frac{715 \text{ words}}{\text{reading time (\quad) sec}} \times 60 = (\qquad) \text{ WPM}$$

Build Your Vocabulary

concentrate ^{복습}
[kánsəntrèit]

v. 집중하다, 집중시키다, 전념하다; **n.** 농축물
If you concentrate on something, you give all your attention to it.

exaggerate [*]
[igzǽdʒərèit]

v. 과장하다
If you exaggerate, you indicate that something is, for example, worse or more important than it really is.

encourage [**]
[inkə́:ridʒ]

v. 격려하다, 용기를 북돋우다
If you encourage someone, you give them confidence, hope, or support.

matter-of-fact
[mǽtər-əv-fǽkt]

a. 사무적인, 무미건조한; 사실의, 실제적인
If you describe a person as matter-of-fact, you mean that they show no emotions such as enthusiasm, anger, or surprise.

stuff ^{복습}
[stʌf]

n. 것(들), 물건, 물질; **v.** 채워 넣다, 속을 채우다
You can use stuff to refer to things such as a substance, a collection of things, events, or ideas, or the contents of something in a general way without mentioning the thing itself by name.

goony
[gú:ni]

a. 어리석은, 미련한; 촌스러운
If you say that someone is goony, you mean they are stupid, foolish, or awkward.

curly ^{복습}
[kə́:rli]

a. 곱슬곱슬한
Curly hair is full of curls.

bald [*]
[bɔ:ld]

a. 대머리의, 머리가 벗겨진
Someone who is bald has little or no hair on the top of their head.

get the idea

idiom 이해하다
If someone gets the idea, they understand how to do something or they understand what you are telling them.

sack ^{복습}
[sæk]

n. 부대, 자루; (쇼핑 물건을 담는 크고 튼튼한 종이) 봉지
A sack is a large bag made of rough woven material.

flour [**]
[fláuər]

n. 밀가루; 분말, 가루
Flour is a white or brown powder that is made by grinding grain, which is used to make bread, cakes, and pastry.

counter [*]
[káuntər]

n. (부엌의) 조리대; 계산대; **v.** 반박하다
A counter is a flat surface in a kitchen which is easy to clean and on which you can prepare food.

80

tip ^{복습}
[tip]

v. 기울어지다, 젖히다; **n.** (뾰족한) 끝
If you tip an object or part of your body or if it tips, it moves into a sloping position with one end or side higher than the other.

burst **
[bə:rst]

v. (burst–burst) 갑자기 ~하다; 터지다, 파열하다; **n.** 폭발, 파열; 돌발
If you burst into tears, laughter, or song, you suddenly begin to cry, laugh, or sing.

figure out ^{복습}

idiom ~을 생각해내다; 계산하다
If you figure out a solution to a problem or the reason for something, you succeed in solving it or understanding it.

strike ^{복습}
[straik]

v. (struck–stricken/struck) 발생하다, 덮치다; 갑자기 떠오르다; 치다, 부딪치다; **n.** 파업; 공격, 공습
If something such as an illness or disaster strikes, it suddenly happens.

trample *
[træmpl]

v. 짓밟다, 밟아 뭉개다, 무시하다; **n.** 쿵쿵거리며 걸음, 짓밟음
If someone tramples something or tramples on it, they step heavily and carelessly on it and damage it.

horoscope
[hɔ́:rəskòup]

n. 점성술, 별점
Your horoscope is a prediction of events which some people believe will happen to you in the future.

logical ^{복습}
[ládʒikəl]

a. 타당한, 사리에 맞는; 논리적인
Something that is logical seems reasonable or sensible in the circumstances.

scientific ^{복습}
[sàiəntífik]

a. 과학적인
Scientific is used to describe things that relate to science or to a particular science.

explanation ^{복습}
[èksplənéiʃən]

n. 해명, 이유; 설명
If you say there is an explanation for something, you mean that there is a reason for it.

ashamed ^{복습}
[əʃéimd]

a. 부끄러워하는
If someone is ashamed, they feel embarrassed or guilty because of something they do or they have done.

cane ^{복습}
[kein]

n. 지팡이
A cane is a long thin stick with a curved or round top which you can use to support yourself when you are walking.

embarrass ^{복습}
[imbǽrəs]

v. 당황스럽게 만들다 (embarrassed **a.** 쑥스러운, 어색한)
If something or someone embarrasses you, they make you feel shy or ashamed.

apologize ^{복습}
[əpálədʒàiz]

v. 사과하다, 사죄하다
When you apologize to someone, you say that you are sorry that you have hurt them or caused trouble for them.

one or the other

idiom 어느 한 쪽, 둘 중 하나
You use one or the other to refer to one or more things or people in a group, when it does not matter which particular one or ones are thought of or chosen.

1분에 몇 단어를 읽는지 리딩 속도를 측정해보세요.

$$\frac{986 \text{ words}}{\text{reading time } (\quad) \text{ sec}} \times 60 = (\quad) \text{ WPM}$$

Build Your Vocabulary

spacey 복습
[spéisi]

a. 멍한
You can use spacey to describe things, especially music, which seem strange, especially because they are very modern or like things in a dream.

witch 복습
[witʃ]

n. 마녀
In fairy stories, a witch is a woman, usually an old woman, who has evil magic powers.

murder**
[mə́:rdər]

v. 죽이다, 살해하다; **n.** 살인
To murder someone means to commit the crime of killing them deliberately.

solution**
[səlú:ʃən]

n. (문제 · 곤경의) 해법, 해결책
A solution to a problem or difficult situation is a way of dealing with it so that the difficulty is removed.

preserve*
[prizə́:rv]

v. 보존하다, 유지하다
If you preserve something, you take action to save it or protect it from damage or decay.

convince*
[kənvíns]

v. 설득하다, 확신시키다, 납득시키다
If someone or something convinces you of something, they make you believe that it is true or that it exists.

blank*
[blæŋk]

a. 빈; 멍한, 무표정한; **n.** 빈칸, 여백
Something that is blank has nothing on it.

regurgitate 복습
[rigə́:rdʒətèit]

v. (삼킨 음식물을 입 안으로 다시) 역류시키다;
(듣거나 읽은 내용을 별 생각 없이) 반복하다
If a person or animal regurgitates food, they bring it back up from their stomach before it has been digested.

creepy
[krí:pi]

a. 소름이 끼치는, 오싹한; 꾸물꾸물 움직이는
If you say that something or someone is creepy, you mean they make you feel very nervous or frightened.

pretend 복습
[priténd]

v. ~인 체하다, 가장하다; **a.** 가짜의, 꾸민
If you pretend that something is the case, you act in a way that is intended to make people believe that it is the case, although in fact it is not.

knock 복습
[nak]

v. 치다, 부수다; (문을) 두드리다, 노크하다
If you knock something, you touch or hit it roughly, especially so that it falls or moves.

toss[*]
[tɔːs]

v. 던지다, 내던지다
If you toss something somewhere, you throw it there lightly, often in a rather careless way.

pitcher 복습
[pítʃər]

① n. 물 주전자 ② n. 투수, 피처
A pitcher is a jug.

horrible 복습
[hɔ́ːrəbl, hɑ́r-]

a. 끔찍한, 소름 끼치게 싫은; 무서운
You can call something horrible when it causes you to feel great shock, fear, and disgust.

guilt[*]
[gilt]

n. 유죄, 죄책감
Guilt is the fact that you have done something wrong or illegal.

pit 복습
[pit]

n. (크고 깊은) 구덩이
A pit is a large hole that is dug in the ground.

bother 복습
[báðər]

v. 귀찮게 하다, 귀찮게 말을 걸다; 신경 쓰다, 애를 쓰다; n. 성가심
If something bothers you, or if you bother about it, it worries, annoys, or upsets you.

weird 복습
[wiərd]

a. 이상한, 기묘한; 수상한
If you describe something or someone as weird, you mean that they are strange.

underpants 복습
[ʌ́ndərpænts]

n. 팬티
Underpants are a piece of underwear which have two holes to put your legs through and elastic around the top to hold them up round your waist or hips.

exclaim 복습
[ikskléim]

v. 외치다, 소리치다
If you exclaim, you say or shout something suddenly because of surprise, fear and pleasure.

crawl 복습
[krɔːl]

v. 기다, 몹시 느리게 가다; n. 기어가기, 서행
When you crawl, you move forward on your hands and knees.

gross[*]
[grous]

a. 역겨운; 총(總)―; 중대한
If you describe something as gross, you think it is very unpleasant.

flip off 복습

idiom 손가락으로 욕을 하다
If you flip someone off, you raise your middle finger to them in a very rude sign.

give someone the bird [finger] 복습

idiom 가운데 손가락을 들어 보이며 모욕하다
If you give someone the bird, you make a rude sign at them with your middle finger.

ghostly 복습
[góustli]

a. 유령 같은; 유령이 많은
Something that is ghostly seems unreal or unnatural and may be frightening because of this.

counterpart 복습
[káuntərpàːrt]

n. 상대, 대응 관계에 있는 사람[것]
Someone's or something's counterpart is another person or thing that has a similar function or position in a different place.

exaggerate 복습
[igzǽdʒərèit]

v. 과장하다

If you exaggerate, you indicate that something is, for example, worse or more important than it really is.

midair
[midέər]

n. 공중, 중천

If something happens in midair, it happens in the air, rather than on the ground.

crash 복습
[kræʃ]

v. 충돌하다, 부딪치다; **n.** (무엇이 떨어지거나 부서질 때 나는) 요란한 소리, 굉음

If something crashes somewhere, it moves and hits something else violently, making a loud noise.

skeptical
[sképtikəl]

a. 회의적인, 의심쩍은

If you are skeptical about something, you have doubts about it.

incident**
[ínsədənt]

n. 일어난 일, 작은 사건

An incident is something that happens, often something that is unpleasant.

coincidence 복습
[kouínsidəns]

n. (우연의) 일치, 부합; 동시에 일어남

A coincidence is when two or more similar or related events occur at the same time by chance and without any planning.

remind 복습
[rimáind]

v. 생각나게 하다, 상기시키다, 일깨우다

If someone reminds you of a fact or event that you already know about, they say something which makes you think about it.

fly 복습
[flai]

n. (바지 앞의) 지퍼로 잠그는 부분; 파리; **v.** (새·곤충이) 날다

The front opening on a pair of trousers is referred to as the fly. It usually consists of a zip or row of buttons behind a band of cloth.

blush 복습
[blʌʃ]

v. 얼굴을 붉히다, 얼굴이 빨개지다; **n.** (당황하거나 수치스러워) 얼굴이 붉어짐

When you blush, your face becomes redder than usual because you are ashamed or embarrassed.

cramp 복습
[kræmp]

① **n.** (근육의) 경련; **v.** 경련을 일으키다, 쥐가 나게 하다 ② **v.** 막다, 방해하다

Cramp is a sudden strong pain caused by a muscle suddenly contracting.

bend 복습
[bend]

v. (bent–bent) 구부리다, 굽히다, 숙이다; **n.** 커브, 굽음, 굽은 곳

When you bend, you move the top part of your body downwards and forwards. Plants and trees also bend.

big deal 복습
[bíg díːl]

int. 그게 무슨 대수라고!; **n.** 대단한 것, 큰 일
(no big deal **int.** 별일 아니다, 대수롭지 않다)

You can say 'big deal' to someone to show that you are not impressed by something that they consider important or impressive.

demonstrate*
[démənstrèit]

v. 실지로 해보이다; 논증하다, 설명하다

If you demonstrate a particular skill, quality, or feeling, you show by your actions that you have it.

gesture 복습
[dʒésʧər]

n. 몸짓; **v.** (손·머리·얼굴 등으로) 가리키다, 몸짓을 하다

A gesture is a movement that you make with a part of your body, especially your hands, to express emotion or information.

idiom 우연히 지나가다
If somebody or something happens by, they appear, arrive, or come casually or by chance.

grab [복습]
[græb]

v. 붙잡다, 움켜잡다; **n.** 움켜잡으려고 함
If you grab something, you take it or pick it up suddenly and roughly.

1. What did Scott say about Tori Williams as he passed by
   David?
   A. He said that Randy should ask her out.
   B. He said that David liked her.
   C. He said that she was hot.
   D. He said that he liked her.

2. What did Larry say about David stepping aside on the
   sidewalk for Scott and Roger?
   A. He said that David did the right thing.
   B. He said that David lost a bet.
   C. He said that David lost face.
   D. He said that David lost respect.

3. Why did Larry say that he didn't have to fight?
   A. He knew karate.
   B. He knew kung fu.
   C. He knew taekwondo.
   D. He knew how to run away.

4. Why was David worried over the weekend?
   A. He was worried about a Spanish test on Monday.
   B. He was worried about Tori dating and liking Randy
   C. He was worried about Larry and Mo not being his friends.
   D. He was worried about how to apologize to Mrs. Bayfield.

5. How did Larry want David to break the curse?
    A. He wanted him to return the cane back to Mrs. Bayfield.
    B. He wanted him to apologize to Mrs. Bayfield.
    C. He wanted him to take a trip to Australia.
    D. He wanted him to pour lemonade on his face.

6. Why was Ricky upset with David?
    A. David always beat Ricky in chess.
    B. David was mean to Ricky's friends.
    C. He thought David was a stooge.
    D. David's friends had teased Ricky.

7. Why did Larry say that he would go on a "pretend" double date?
    A. He wanted Mo to be his girlfriend.
    B. He wanted to see a scary movie.
    C. He wanted to be popular.
    D. He wanted to help out David.

Check Your Reading Speed

1분에 몇 단어를 읽는지 리딩 속도를 측정해보세요.

$$\frac{979 \text{ words}}{\text{reading time } (\quad) \text{ sec}} \times 60 = (\qquad) \text{ WPM}$$

Build Your Vocabulary

abrupt ^{복습}
[əbrʌ́pt]

a. 갑작스러운, 뜻밖의; 퉁명스러운 (abruptly **ad.** 갑자기)
An abrupt change or action is very sudden, often in a way which is unpleasant.

sidewalk ^{복습}
[sáidwɔ:k]

n. (포장한) 보도, 인도
A sidewalk is a path with a hard surface by the side of a road.

glance ^{복습}
[glæns]

v. 흘긋 보다, 잠깐 보다; **n.** 흘긋 봄
If you glance at something or someone, you look at them very quickly and then look away again immediately.

equal ^{복습}
[í:kwəl]

a. (수 · 양 · 가치등이)동일한;동등한, 평등한; **v.** (수 · 양 · 가치등이)같다, ~이다 (equally **ad.** 똑같이, 동일하게)
If two things are equal or if one thing is equal to another, they are the same in size, number, standard, or value.

for one's benefit

idiom ~를 위해
If you say that someone is doing something for someone's benefit, you mean that they are doing it for that person.

jerk ^{복습}
[dʒə:rk]

① **n.** 바보, 멍청이 ② **v.** 홱 움직이다; **n.** (갑자기 날카롭게) 홱 움직임
If you call someone a jerk, you are insulting them because you think they are stupid or you do not like them.

push someone around ^{복습}

idiom ~에게 마구 이래라저래라 하다
If you push someone around, you order them to do things in a threatening or unpleasant way.

rub ^{복습}
[rʌb]

v. 비비다, 문지르다; 스치다; **n.** 문지르기
If you rub a part of your body, you move your hand or fingers backwards and forwards over it while pressing firmly.

chop *
[tʃap]

v. 내려치다; (음식 재료를 토막으로) 썰다; **n.** 토막; 내리치기
If you chop, you make a short quick downward stroke.

curse ^{복습}
[kə:rs]

n. 저주; 욕(설), 악담; **v.** 욕(설)을 하다; 저주를 내리다
If you say that there is a curse on someone, you mean that there seems to be a supernatural power causing unpleasant things to happen to them.

shrug ^{복습}
[ʃrʌg]

v. (양 손바닥을 내보이면서 어깨를) 으쓱하다; **n.** (어깨를) 으쓱하기
If you shrug, you raise your shoulders to show that you are not interested in something or that you do not know or care about something.

earthquake
[ə́:rθkwèik]

n. 지진
An earthquake is a shaking of the ground caused by movement of the earth's crust.

force***
[fɔ:rs]

v. (미소 등을) 억지로 짓다; (〜을 하도록) 〜를 강요하다; n. 물리력, 폭력
If you force a smile or a laugh, you manage to smile or laugh, but with an effort because you are unhappy.

tear^{복습}
[ter]

① v. (tore–torn) 찢다, 찢어지다; n. 찢음 ② n. 눈물
If you tear paper, cloth, or another material, or if it tears, you pull it into two pieces or you pull it so that a hole appears in it.

1분에 몇 단어를 읽는지 리딩 속도를 측정해보세요.

$$\frac{1{,}785 \text{ words}}{\text{reading time (}\quad\text{) sec}} \times 60 = (\quad) \text{ WPM}$$

Build Your Vocabulary

rate[**]
[reit]

v. 등급[순위]을 매기다; 평가하다; **n.** 속도; 비율
If someone or something is rated at a particular position or rank, they are calculated or considered to be in that position on a list.

curly[복습]
[kə́:rli]

a. 곱슬곱슬한
Curly hair is full of curls.

shawl
[ʃɔ:l]

n. 숄
A shawl is a large piece of woollen cloth which a woman wears over her shoulders or head, or which is wrapped around a baby to keep it warm.

flash[복습]
[flæʃ]

v. (잠깐) 비치다, 번쩍이다; 비추다; (분노 등으로) 발끈[폭발]하다 **n.** 섬광, 번쩍임
If a light flashes or if you flash a light, it shines with a sudden bright light, especially as quick, regular flashes of light.

breeze[*]
[bri:z]

v. 거침없이[경쾌하게] 움직이다; **n.** 산들바람, 미풍
If you breeze into a place or a position, you enter it in a very casual or relaxed manner.

ease[**]
[i:z]

v. 천천히 움직이다; (고통·고민 등을) 진정[완화]시키다; **n.** 편함, 안정
If you ease your way somewhere or ease somewhere, you move there slowly, carefully, and gently. If you ease something somewhere, you move it there slowly, carefully, and gently.

on the other hand

idiom 다른 한편으로는, 반면에
You use on the other hand to introduce the second of two contrasting points, facts, or ways of looking at something.

effort[***]
[éfərt]

n. 노력, 수고
If you make an effort to do something, you try very hard to do it

big deal[복습]
[bíg dí:l]

int. 그게 무슨 대수라고!; **n.** 대단한 것, 큰 일
You can say 'big deal' to someone to show that you are not impressed by something that they consider important or impressive.

chide
[tʃaid]

v. 꾸짖다, 비난하다
If you chide someone, you speak to them angrily because they have done something wicked or foolish.

thumb[복습]
[θʌm]

v. (책을) 엄지손가락으로 넘기다; **n.** 엄지손가락
If you thumb through a book, magazine, or a document, you to turn the pages of it quickly and only read small parts of it.

cane ^{복습}
[kein]

n. 지팡이
A cane is a long thin stick with a curved or round top which you can use to support yourself when you are walking.

better late than never

idiom 하지 않는 것보다는 늦더라도 하는 것이 낫다
If you say better late than never when someone has done something, you think they should have done it earlier.

figure out ^{복습}

idiom ~을 생각해내다; 계산하다
If you figure out a solution to a problem or the reason for something, you succeed in solving it or understanding it.

recess ^{복습}
[risés]

n. (학교의) 쉬는 시간; 휴회
A recess is a short period of time when you have a rest or a change from what you are doing, especially if you are working or if you are in a boring or unpleasant situation.

mutter ^{복습}
[mʌ́tər]

v. 중얼거리다; 투덜거리다; **n.** 중얼거림
If you mutter, you speak very quietly so that you cannot easily be heard, often because you are complaining about something.

go[come] full circle

idiom (한 바퀴 돌아) 제 자리로 되돌아오다
If you say that you have gone full circle, you mean that after a long series of events or changes the same situation that you started with still exists.

protest ^{**}
[próutest]

v. 항의하다, 이의를 제기하다; **n.** 항의
If you protest against something or about something, you say or show publicly that you object to it.

dump ^{복습}
[dʌmp]

v. 쏟아 버리다, 내버리다, 아무렇게나 내려놓다; **n.** 쓰레기 더미
If you dump something somewhere, you put it or unload it there quickly and carelessly.

witness ^{**}
[wítnis]

n. 목격자, 증인; **v.** 목격하다; 증언하다
A witness to an event such as an accident or crime is a person who saw it.

ridiculous ^{**}
[ridíkjuləs]

a. 웃기는, 말도 안 되는, 터무니없는
If you say that something or someone is ridiculous, you mean that they are very foolish.

guarantee [*]
[gærəntí:]

n. 보증, 개런티; **v.** 보증하다, 다짐하다
Something that is a guarantee of something else makes it certain that it will happen or that it is true.

cure ^{복습}
[kjuər]

v. (사람·동물을 아프지 않도록) 낫게 하다; **n.** 치유하는 약, 치유법
If doctors or medical treatments cure a person, they make the person well again after an illness or injury.

give me a break

idiom 그만 좀 해! 적당히 해!
You can say 'give me a break' to show that you are annoyed by what someone has said or done.

freezer [*]
[frí:zər]

n. 냉동고
A freezer is a large container like a fridge in which the temperature is kept below freezing point so that you can store food inside it for long periods.

concentrate ^{복습}
[kánsəntrèit]

n. 농축물; **v.** 집중하다, 집중시키다, 전념하다
Concentrate is a liquid or substance from which water has been removed in order to make it stronger, or to make it easier to store.

expert *
[ékspə:rt]

n. 전문가; **a.** 숙련된, 노련한
An expert is a person who is very skilled at doing something or who knows a lot about a particular subject.

chin **
[tʃin]

n. 턱
Your chin is the part of your face that is below your mouth and above your neck.

declare ^{복습}
[diklɛ́ər]

v. 선언하다; 단언하다
If you declare something, you state officially and formally that it exists or is the case.

disbelief
[dìsbilíːf]

n. 믿기지 않음, 불신감
Disbelief is not believing that something is true or real.

peel ^{복습}
[piːl]

v. 벗겨지다, 껍질을 벗기다
If a surface is peeling, the paint on it is coming away.

content ^{복습}
[kəntént]

① **n.** (pl.) (어떤 것의) 속에 든 것들, 내용물; 목차
② **a.** (자기가 가진 것에) 만족하는; **v.** ~에 자족하다
The contents of a container such as a bottle, box, or room are the things that are inside it.

blender
[bléndər]

n. 믹서기, 분쇄기(요리 기구)
A blender is an electrical kitchen appliance used for mixing liquids and soft foods together or turning fruit or vegetables into liquid.

stare ^{복습}
[stɛər]

v. 빤히 쳐다보다, 응시하다; **n.** 빤히 쳐다보기, 응시
If you stare at someone or something, you look at them for a long time.

convince ^{복습}
[kənvíns]

v. 설득하다, 확신시키다, 납득시키다
If someone or something convinces you of something, they make you believe that it is true or that it exists.

lean ^{복습}
[liːn]

v. ~에 기대다; 기울이다, (몸을) 숙이다
If you lean on or against someone or something, you rest against them so that they partly support your weight.

circumstance **
[sə́:rkəmstæns]

n. 상황, 환경, 사정
The circumstances of a particular situation are the conditions which affect what happens.

bomb ^{복습}
[bam]

n. 폭탄; **v.** 폭탄으로 공격하다, 폭격하다
A bomb is a device which explodes and damages or destroys a large area.

squad *
[skwad]

n. 분대, 소집단 (bomb squad **n.** 폭탄 처리반)
A squad of soldiers is a small group of them.

explode ^{복습}
[iksplóud]

v. 폭발하다, 격발하다; 폭발시키다
If someone explodes, they express strong feelings suddenly and violently.

foam[*]
[foum]

n. (액체 표면에 생긴) 거품 (foamy **a.** 거품이 있는)
Foam consists of a mass of small bubbles that are formed when air and a liquid are mixed together.

steady[**]
[stédi]

a. 흔들림 없는, 안정된; (발달 · 전개 등이) 꾸준한; **v.** (흔들리지 않게) 균형을 잡다
If an object is steady, it is firm and does not shake or move about.

tip[복습]
[tip]

v. 기울어지다, 젖히다; **n.** (뾰족한) 끝
If you tip an object or part of your body or if it tips, it moves into a sloping position with one end or side higher than the other.

splatter
[splǽtər]

v. 튀다, 튀기다; **n.** 튀기기; 철벅철벅 소리
If a thick wet substance splatters on something or is splattered on it, it drops or is thrown over it.

forehead[*]
[fɔ́:rhèd]

n. 이마
Your forehead is the area at the front of your head between your eyebrows and your hair.

crack up[복습]

idiom 마구 웃기 시작하다
If you crack up, you suddenly start laughing a lot.

sticky[*]
[stíki]

a. 끈적[끈끈]한, 들러붙는, 점착성의
A sticky substance is soft, or thick and liquid, and can stick to other things.

period[복습]
[píːəriəd]

n. 기간, 시기; (학교의 일과를 나눠 놓은) 시간; (여성의) 생리
A period is a length of time.

strike[복습]
[straik]

v. 발생하다, 덮치다; 갑자기 떠오르다; 치다, 부딪치다; **n.** 파업; 공격, 공습
If something such as an illness or disaster strikes, it suddenly happens.

1분에 몇 단어를 읽는지 리딩 속도를 측정해보세요.

$$\frac{1{,}985 \text{ words}}{\text{reading time } (\quad) \text{ sec}} \times 60 = (\quad) \text{ WPM}$$

Build Your Vocabulary

blender^{복습}
[bléndər]

n. 믹서기, 분쇄기(요리 기구)
A blender is an electrical kitchen appliance used for mixing liquids and soft foods together or turning fruit or vegetables into liquid.

counter^{복습}
[káuntər]

n. (부엌의) 조리대; 계산대; **v.** 반박하다
A counter is a flat surface in a kitchen which is easy to clean and on which you can prepare food.

bury**
[béri]

v. 묻다, 파묻다, 매장하다
If you bury your head or face in something, you press your head or face against it, often because you are unhappy.

pitcher^{복습}
[pítʃər]

① **n.** 물 주전자 ② **n.** 투수, 피처
A pitcher is a jug.

sink^{복습}
[siŋk]

n. (부엌의) 싱크대, 개수대; **v.** 가라앉다, 빠지다
A sink is a large fixed container in a kitchen, with taps to supply water. It is mainly used for washing dishes.

jerk^{복습}
[dʒəːrk]

① **v.** 확 움직이다; **n.** (갑자기 날카롭게) 확 움직임 ② **n.** 바보, 멍청이
If you jerk something or someone in a particular direction, or they jerk in a particular direction, they move a short distance very suddenly and quickly.

swollen
[swóulən]

a. 부어오른, 부푼
If a part of your body is swollen, it is larger and rounder than normal, usually as a result of injury or illness.

bruise*
[bruːz]

v. 멍들게 하다, 타박상을 입히다; **n.** 타박상, 멍 (bruised **a.** 멍든)
If you bruise a part of your body, a bruise appears on it, for example because something hits you. If you bruise easily, bruises appear when something hits you only slightly.

yell^{복습}
[jel]

v. 소리치다, 고함치다; **n.** 고함소리, 부르짖음
If you yell, you shout loudly, usually because you are excited, angry, or in pain.

build someone up

idiom ~을 과대 포장하다
If you build someone up, you speak about them with great enthusiasm, often praising them more than they deserve.

sooner or later

idiom 조만간, 머지않아
If you say that something will happen sooner or later, you mean that it will happen at some time in the future, even though it might take a long time.

94

slip ^{복습}
[slip]

v. (어떤 위치 · 손을 벗어나) 미끄러지다, 빠져 나가다; (재빨리 · 슬며시) 놓다;
n. (작은 종이) 조각, 쪽지
If something slips, it slides out of place or out of your hand.

get rid of

idiom ~을 없애다, 제거하다, 처리하다
If you get rid of somebody or something, you make yourself free of somebody or something that is annoying you or that you do not want or you throw something away.

pretend ^{복습}
[priténd]

v. ~인 체하다, 가장하다; a. 가짜의, 꾸민
If you pretend that something is the case, you act in a way that is intended to make people believe that it is the case, although in fact it is not.

complicate＊
[kámplikèit]

v. (더) 복잡하게 만들다
To complicate something means to make it more difficult to understand or deal with.

squint
[skwint]

v. 실눈으로 보다, 곁눈질을 하다; a. 사시의; 곁눈질하는
If you squint at something, you look at it with your eyes partly closed.

couch＊
[kautʃ]

n. 소파, 긴 의자
A couch is a long, comfortable seat for two or three people.

den＊
[den]

n. 편안히 쉴 수 있는 방; (야생 동물이 사는) 굴
Your den is a quiet room in your house where you can go to study, work, or carry on a hobby without being disturbed.

block ^{복습}
[blak]

v. (지나가지 못하게) 막다, 차단하다; n. 사각형 덩어리; 구역, 블록
If you block someone's way, you prevent them from going somewhere or entering a place by standing in front of them.

rerun
[rìrʌ́n]

v. 재방송, 재상영; 재경주, 재시합; v. 재방송하다, 재상영하다
A rerun is a film, play, or television program that is shown or put on again.

device＊
[diváis]

n. 장치, 설비
A device is a machine or tool that does a special job.

neat ^{복습}
[ni:t]

a. 뛰어난, 훌륭한; 정돈된, 단정한, 말쑥한
If you say that something is neat, you mean that it is very good.

exclaim ^{복습}
[ikskléim]

v. 외치다, 소리치다
If you exclaim, you say or shout something suddenly because of surprise, fear and pleasure.

slam ^{복습}
[slæm]

v. 세게 놓다; 쾅[탁] 닫다
If you slam something down, you put it there quickly and with great force.

snap ^{복습}
[snæp]

v. (화난 목소리로) 딱딱거리다; 딱[툭] (하고) 부러뜨리다; n. 찰칵 하는 소리
If someone snaps at you, they speak to you in a sharp, unfriendly way.

radical＊
[rǽdikəl]

a. 기막히게 좋은, 끝내 주는; 근본적인, 철저한; 급진적인, 과격한
If you say that something is radical, it means very good or excellent.

churn
[tʃə:rn]

v. (속이) 뒤틀리다; (물 · 파도 등이) 마구 휘돌다, 휘젓다; 거품이 나게 하다
If you say that your stomach is churning, you mean that you feel sick.

delight ^{복습}
[diláit]

v. 많은 기쁨을 주다, 아주 즐겁게 하다; **n.** (큰) 기쁨
(delighted a. 아주 기뻐하는)
If you are delighted, you are extremely pleased and excited about something.

bounce ^{복습}
[bauns]

v. 튀다, 튀게 하다; 급히 움직이다, 뛰어다니다; **n.** 튐, 바운드
If something bounces off a surface or is bounced off it, it reaches the surface and is reflected back.

independent **
[indipéndənt]

a. 독립한, 자치적인, 독립심이 강한 (independence **n.** 독립)
If one thing or person is independent of another, they are separate and not connected, so the first one is not affected or influenced by the second

pursue *
[pərsú:]

v. 쫓다, 추구하다 (pursuit **n.** 추구)
If you pursue a particular topic, you try to find out more about it.

hardly ^{복습}
[há:rdli]

ad. 거의 ~아니다, 전혀 ~않다
When you say you can hardly do something, you are emphasizing that it is very difficult for you to do it.

make sense ^{복습}

idiom 의미가 통하다, 말이 되다; 이해[설명]하기 쉽다
If something makes sense, it has a meaning that you can easily understand.

cigarette ^{복습}
[sigərét]

n. 담배
Cigarettes are small tubes of paper containing tobacco which people smoke.

illegal *
[ilí:gəl]

a. 불법의, 비합법적인
If something is illegal, the law says that it is not allowed.

severe **
[sivíər]

a. 극심한, 심각한
You use severe to indicate that something bad or undesirable is great or intense.

criminal ^{복습}
[krímənl]

n. 범죄자, 범인
A criminal is a person who regularly commits crimes.

trash ^{복습}
[træʃ]

n. 쓰레기; **v.** 부수다, 엉망으로 만들다
Trash consists of unwanted things or waste material such as used paper, empty containers and bottles, and waste food.

robber *
[rábər]

n. 강도, 도둑
A robber is someone who steals money or property from a bank, a shop, or a vehicle, often by using force or threats.

murder ^{복습}
[mə́:rdər]

v. 죽이다, 살해하다; **n.** 살인 (murderer **n.** 살인범)
To murder someone means to commit the crime of killing them deliberately.

shoplift
[ʃáplift]

v. 가게 물건을 훔치다 (shoplifter **n.** 가게 좀도둑)
If someone shoplifts, they steal goods from a shop by hiding them in a bag or in their clothes.

obvious ^{복습}
[ábviəs]

a. 명백한, 분명한 (obviously **ad.** 분명히, 명백하게)
If something is obvious, it is easy to see or understand.

period^{복습}
[píːəriəd]

n. 기간, 시기; (학교의 일과를 나눠 놓은) 시간; (여성의) 생리
A period is a length of time.

odd^{복습}
[ad]

a. 이상한, 특이한
If you describe someone or something as odd, you think that they are strange or unusual.

blush^{복습}
[blʌʃ]

v. 얼굴을 붉히다, 얼굴이 빨개지다; **n.** (당황하거나 수치스러워) 얼굴이 붉어짐
When you blush, your face becomes redder than usual because you are ashamed or embarrassed.

dread[*]
[dred]

v. 몹시 무서워하다, 두려워하다; **n.** 두려움; 두려운 것
If you dread something which may happen, you feel very anxious and unhappy about it because you think it will be unpleasant or upsetting.

vulnerable[*]
[vʌ́lnərəbl]

a. 상처를 입기 쉬운, 공격받기 쉬운
Weak and easily hurt physically or emotionally.

constant[*]
[kánstənt]

a. 일정한, 불변의, 끊임없는 (constantly **ad.** 일정하게, 끊임없이, 지속적으로)
You use constant to describe something that happens all the time or is always there.

sweat^{복습}
[swet]

v. 땀 흘리다; 습기가 차다; **n.** 땀
When you sweat, drops of liquid comes through your skin.

splash[*]
[splæʃ]

v. (물·흙탕 등) 튀(기)다, 첨벙거리다; **n.** 첨벙 튀기는 소리
If you splash a liquid somewhere or if it splashes, it hits someone or something and scatters in a lot of small drops.

gut
[gʌt]

n. (pl.) 배짱; 소화관; (사람의) 배
Guts is the will and courage to do something which is difficult or unpleasant, or which might have unpleasant results.

comb^{복습}
[koum]

v. 빗다, 빗질하다; **n.** 빗(질)
When you comb your hair, you tidy it using a flat piece of plastic or metal with narrow pointed teeth along one side.

spot^{**}
[spat]

v. 발견하다, 분별하다; **n.** 장소, 지점; 반점, 얼룩
If you spot something or someone, you notice them.

beat^{복습}
[biːt]

v. 때리다, 두드리다; (게임·시합에서) 이기다; (심장이) 고동치다; **n.** 고동, 맥박
If you beat someone or something, you hit them very hard.

pound^{복습}
[paund]

① **v.** 쿵쿵 울리다, 마구 치다, 세게 두드리다; **n.** 타격 ② **n.** 파운드(무게의 단위)
③ **n.** 주인 잃은 개 보호소
If you pound something or pound on it, you hit it with great force, usually loudly and repeatedly.

toss^{복습}
[tɔːs]

v. 던지다, 내던지다
If you toss something somewhere, you throw it there lightly, often in a rather careless way.

roof^{복습}
[ruːf]

n. 지붕
The roof of a building is the covering on top of it that protects the people and things inside from the weather.

momentary[*]
[móuməntèri]

a. 찰나의, 순식간의 (momentarily **ad.** 잠깐)
Something that is momentary lasts for a very short period of time.

lunge
[lʌndʒ]

v. (사람을 공격하거나 무엇을 움켜잡으려고) 달려들다, 돌진하다; n. 돌진
If you lunge in a particular direction, you move in that direction suddenly and clumsily.

v. (사람을 공격하거나 무엇을 움켜잡으려고) 달려들다, 돌진하다; **n.** 돌진
If you lunge in a particular direction, you move in that direction suddenly and clumsily.

1분에 몇 단어를 읽는지 리딩 속도를 측정해보세요.

$$\frac{1,300 \text{ words}}{\text{reading time } (\quad) \text{ sec}} \times 60 = (\quad) \text{ WPM}$$

Build Your Vocabulary

slide^{복습}
[slaid]

v. (slid–slid) 미끄러지다, 미끄러지듯 움직이다
If you slide somewhere, you move there smoothly and quietly.

spill^{복습}
[spil]

v. 엎지르다, 흘리다; **n.** 엎지름, 유출
If a liquid spills or if you spill it, it accidentally flows over the edge of a container.

ignore^{복습}
[ignɔ́:r]

v. 무시하다
If you ignore someone or something, you pay no attention to them.

curse^{복습}
[kə:rs]

n. 저주; 욕(설), 악담; **v.** 욕(설)을 하다; 저주를 내리다
If you say that there is a curse on someone, you mean that there seems to be a supernatural power causing unpleasant things to happen to them.

insist^{복습}
[insíst]

v. 우기다, 주장하다; 강요하다
If you insist that something is the case, you say so very firmly and refuse to say otherwise, even though other people do not believe you.

criminal^{복습}
[krímənl]

n. 범죄자, 범인
A criminal is a person who regularly commits crimes.

trash^{복습}
[træʃ]

n. 쓰레기; **v.** 부수다, 엉망으로 만들다
Trash consists of unwanted things or waste material such as used paper, empty containers and bottles, and waste food.

scary
[skɛ́əri]

a. 무서운, 두려운
Something that is scary is rather frightening.

robber^{복습}
[rábər]

n. 강도, 도둑
A robber is someone who steals money or property from a bank, a shop, or a vehicle, often by using force or threats.

murder^{복습}
[mə́:rdər]

v. 죽이다, 살해하다; **n.** 살인 (murderer **n.** 살인범)
To murder someone means to commit the crime of killing them deliberately.

horrible^{복습}
[hɔ́:rəbl]

a. 끔찍한, 소름 끼치게 싫은; 무서운
You can call something horrible when it causes you to feel great shock, fear, and disgust.

grin^{**}
[grin]

v. (이를 드러내고) 싱긋 웃다, 활짝 웃다; **n.** 싱긋 웃음
When you grin, you smile broadly.

bush^{복습}
[buʃ]

n. 관목, 덤불
A bush is a large plant which is smaller than a tree and has a lot of branches.

weird^{복습}
[wiərd]

a. 이상한, 기묘한; 수상한
If you describe something or someone as weird, you mean that they are strange.

frighten**
[fráitn]

v. 놀라게 하다, 섬뜩하게 하다; 기겁하다 (frightened a. 놀란, 섬뜩한, 기겁한)
If something or someone frightens you, they cause you to suddenly feel afraid, anxious, or nervous.

laboratory^{복습}
[lǽbərətɔ̀:ri]

n. (= lab) 실험실, 연구실
A laboratory is a building or a room where scientific experiments, analyses, and research are carried out.

equipment**
[ikwípmənt]

n. 장비, 설비
Equipment consists of the things which are used for a particular purpose, for example a hobby or job.

chemical^{복습}
[kémikəl]

n. 화학 물질; a. 화학의
Chemicals are substances that are used in a chemical process or made by a chemical process.

warn^{복습}
[wɔ:rn]

v. 경고하다, 주의를 주다, 조심하라고 하다
If you warn someone about something such as a possible danger or problem, you tell them about it so that they are aware of it.

adjust**
[ədʒʌ́st]

v. (옷매무새 등을) 바로 하다; 조절하다, 조정하다
If you adjust something such as your clothing or a machine, you correct or alter its position or setting.

signal^{복습}
[sígnəl]

v. (동작·소리로) 신호를 보내다; n. (동작·소리로 하는) 신호
If you signal to someone, you make a gesture or sound in order to send them a particular message.

grip**
[grip]

v. 꽉 잡다, 움켜잡다; n. 잡음, 움켜쥠; 손잡이
If you grip something, you take hold of it with your hand and continue to hold it firmly.

count**
[kaunt]

v. (정식으로) 인정되다; 수를 세다, 계산하다; 중요하다; n. 셈, 계산
If something counts or is counted as a particular thing, it is regarded as being that thing, especially in particular circumstances or under particular rules.

remind^{복습}
[rimáind]

v. 생각나게 하다, 상기시키다, 일깨우다
If someone reminds you of a fact or event that you already know about, they say something which makes you think about it.

stick with someone

idiom ~의 곁에 머물다
If you stick with someone, you stay physically close to them.

cheat**
[tʃi:t]

v. 속이다; 규칙을 어기다; n. 사기
To behave in a dishonest way in order to get what you want.

protest^{복습}
[próutest]

v. 항의하다, 이의를 제기하다; n. 항의
If you protest against something or about something, you say or show publicly that you object to it.

rack ^{복습}
[ræk]

n. 받침대, 선반
A rack is a frame or shelf, usually with bars or hooks, that is used for holding things or for hanging things on.

abrupt ^{복습}
[əbrʌpt]

a. 갑작스러운, 뜻밖의; 퉁명스러운 (abruptly **ad.** 갑자기)
An abrupt change or action is very sudden, often in a way which is unpleasant.

coincidence ^{복습}
[kouínsidəns]

n. (우연의) 일치, 부합; 동시에 일어남
A coincidence is when two or more similar or related events occur at the same time by chance and without any planning.

jerk ^{복습}
[dʒə:rk]

① **n.** 바보, 멍청이 ② **v.** 홱 움직이다; **n.** (갑자기 날카롭게) 홱 움직임
If you call someone a jerk, you are insulting them because you think they are stupid or you do not like them.

subtle *
[sʌtl]

a. 미묘한, 미세한; 교묘한, 솜씨 좋은
Something that is subtle is not immediately obvious or noticeable.

scowl
[skaul]

v. 얼굴을 찌푸리다, 싫은 기색을 하다; **n.** 찌푸린 얼굴
When someone scowls, an angry or hostile expression appears on their face.

flush ^{복습}
[flʌʃ]

v. (변기의) 물을 내리다; (얼굴 등을) 붉히다; **n.** (볼 등의) 홍조
When someone flushes a toilet after using it, they fill the toilet bowl with water in order to clean it, usually by pressing a handle or pulling a chain.

fly ^{복습}
[flai]

n. (바지 앞의) 지퍼[단추]로 잠그는 부분; 파리; **v.** (새 · 곤충이) 날다
The front opening on a pair of trousers is referred to as the fly. It usually consists of a zip or row of buttons behind a band of cloth.

escort *
[éskɔ:rt]

v. 호송하다; 호위하다, 동행하다; **n.** 호위, 호송
If you escort someone somewhere, you accompany them there.

prisoner **
[prízənər]

n. 죄수, 포로
A prisoner is a person who is kept in a prison as a punishment for a crime that they have committed.

ceiling **
[sí:liŋ]

n. 천장
A ceiling is the horizontal surface that forms the top part or roof inside a room.

roof ^{복습}
[ru:f]

n. 지붕
The roof of a building is the covering on top of it that protects the people and things inside from the weather.

cave in

idiom (지붕 · 벽 등이) 무너지다, 함몰되다
If a roof or wall caves in, it falls down and towards the center.

1. Why did David decide not to call Tori after looking at the phone book?
   A. He was too nervous to talk to her.
   B. He couldn't find her number.
   C. His phone was broken.
   D. He thought that she was dating Randy.

2. What did David do for good luck on Friday morning?
   A. He walked to school with Larry and Mo.
   B. He brought a lucky charm in his pocket.
   C. He put on his best and luckiest clothes.
   D. He made breakfast for his family.

3. Why did David think that the curse was back?
   A. He broke the remote control while watching television.
   B. He spilled apple juice on Elizabeth's face.
   C. He broke his bedroom window with a ball.
   D. He spilled water over his homework.

4. What did Tori say that David looked like?
   A. A Greek poet
   B. A French artist
   C. A British businessman
   D. A stooge

5. What did David think were the eeriest masks hanging in
   Mrs. Bayfield's living room?
   A. The ones with three eyes
   B. The ones that looked like real faces
   C. The ones that were part human and part animal
   D. The ones that were half black and half white

6. Why did David go to Roger's house after leaving Mrs.
   Bayfield's home?
   A. He wanted to talk to Roger about Mrs. Bayfield.
   B. He wanted to get revenge on Glen for Ricky.
   C. He wanted to steal the cane back.
   D. He wanted to fight Roger for the cane.

7. Why did David not fight Glen?
   A. He didn't want to fight a little kid.
   B. He didn't want to make Roger angry.
   C. He was afraid of Glen.
   D. He didn't want to get sweaty.

1분에 몇 단어를 읽는지 리딩 속도를 측정해보세요.

$$\frac{1,010 \text{ words}}{\text{reading time (} \quad \text{) sec}} \times 60 = (\quad) \text{ WPM}$$

Build Your Vocabulary

convince ^{복습}
[kənvíns]

v. 설득하다, 확신시키다, 납득시키다
If someone or something convinces you of something, they make you believe that it is true or that it exists.

chicken out

idiom 겁을 먹고 (~을) 그만두다
If you chicken out, you decide not to do something because you are afraid.

bother ^{복습}
[báðər]

v. 신경 쓰다, 애를 쓰다; 귀찮게 하다, 귀찮게 말을 걸다; n. 성가심
If you do not bother to do something or if you do not bother with it, you do not do it, consider it, or use it because you think it is unnecessary or because you are too lazy.

spontaneous
[spantéiniəs]

a. (사람이) 즉흥적인; 자발적인, 마음에서 우러난
Spontaneous acts are not planned or arranged, but are done because someone suddenly wants to do them.

peer *
[piər]

n. (나이 · 신분이 같거나 비슷한) 또래; v. 응시하다, 자세히 보다
(peer pressure n. 동료 집단으로부터 받는 사회적 압력)
Your peers are the people who are the same age as you or who have the same status as you.

drug ^{복습}
[drʌg]

n. (불법적인) 약물, 마약; 의약품, 약
Drugs are substances that some people take because of their pleasant effects, but which are usually illegal.

thumb ^{복습}
[θʌm]

v. (책을) 엄지손가락으로 넘기다; n. 엄지손가락
If you thumb through a book, magazine, or a document, you to turn the pages of it quickly and only read small parts of it.

delight ^{복습}
[diláit]

v. 많은 기쁨을 주다, 아주 즐겁게 하다; n. (큰) 기쁨
(delighted a. 아주 기뻐[즐거워]하는)
If you are delighted, you are extremely pleased and excited about something.

consent *
[kənsént]

v. 동의하다, 허락하다; n. (권위 있는 사람에 의한) 동의, 허락
If you consent to something, you agree to do it or to allow it to be done.

reject
[ridʒékt]

v. (주장 · 생각 · 계획 등을) 거부하다, 거절하다
If you reject something such as a proposal, a request, or an offer, you do not accept it or you do not agree to it.

den 복습
[den]

n. 편안히 쉴 수 있는 방; (야생 동물이 사는) 굴
Your den is a quiet room in your house where you can go to study, work, or carry on a hobby without being disturbed.

scowl 복습
[skaul]

v. 얼굴을 찌푸리다, 싫은 기색을 하다; n. 찌푸린 얼굴
When someone scowls, an angry or hostile expression appears on their face.

sarcastic*
[sa:rkǽstik]

a. 빈정대는, 비꼬는, 풍자적인 (sarcastically ad. 비꼬는 투로, 풍자적으로)
Someone who is sarcastic says or does the opposite of what they really mean in order to mock or insult someone.

block 복습
[blak]

n. 사각형 덩어리; 구역, 블록; v. (지나가지 못하게) 막다, 차단하다
A block of a substance is a large rectangular piece of it.

circular*
[sə́:rkjulər]

a. 원형의, 둥근; 순회하는
Something that is circular is shaped like a circle.

clap*
[klæp]

v. 박수를 치다, 손뼉을 치다; n. 박수
When you clap, you hit your hands together to show appreciation or attract attention.

shrug 복습
[ʃrʌg]

v. (양 손바닥을 내보이면서 어깨를) 으쓱하다; n. (어깨를) 으쓱하기
If you shrug, you raise your shoulders to show that you are not interested in something or that you do not know or care about something.

mutter 복습
[mʌ́tər]

v. 중얼거리다; 투덜거리다; n. 중얼거림
If you mutter, you speak very quietly so that you cannot easily be heard, often because you are complaining about something.

refrigerator*
[rifrídʒərèitər]

n. 냉장고
A refrigerator is a large container which is kept cool inside, usually by electricity, so that the food and drink in it stays fresh.

make up for 복습

idiom ~에 대해 보상하다, (잘못된 상황을 바로잡을 수 있도록) 만회하다
If you make up for something, you do something good for someone because you have treated them badly or because they have done something good for you.

suffer 복습
[sʌ́fər]

v. (질병 · 고통 · 슬픔 · 결핍 등에) 시달리다, 고통받다
If you suffer pain, you feel it in your body or in your mind.

helpless 복습
[hélplis]

a. 무력한, 속수무책의 (helplessly ad. 무력하게, 어쩔 수 없이)
If you are helpless, you do not have the strength or power to do anything useful or to control or protect yourself.

take the chill off

idiom 조금 데우다
If you take the chill off something, you make it slightly less cold.

nipple
[nipl]

n. (고무로 된) 젖꼭지
A nipple is a piece of rubber or plastic which is fitted to the top of a baby's bottle.

1분에 몇 단어를 읽는지 리딩 속도를 측정해보세요.

$$\frac{1,513 \text{ words}}{\text{reading time (}\qquad\text{) sec}} \times 60 = (\qquad) \text{ WPM}$$

Build Your Vocabulary

nipple 복습
[nipl]

n. (고무로 된) 젖꼭지
A nipple is a piece of rubber or plastic which is fitted to the top of a baby's bottle.

witch 복습
[witʃ]

n. 마녀
In fairy stories, a witch is a woman, usually an old woman, who has evil magic powers.

doorway 복습
[dɔ́:rwèi]

n. 출입구
A doorway is a space in a wall where a door opens and closes.

baggy
[bǽgi]

a. 자루 같은, 헐렁한, 불룩한
If a piece of clothing is baggy, it hangs loosely on your body.

drawstring
[drɔ́:striŋ]

n. (가방 · 바지 등을) 졸라매는 끈
A drawstring is a cord that goes through an opening, for example at the top of a bag or a pair of trousers.

sleeve*
[sli:v]

n. (옷의) 소매, 소맷자락
The sleeves of a coat, shirt, or other item of clothing are the parts that cover your arms.

horizontal*
[hɔ̀:rəzántl]

a. 수평(선)의, 가로의; **n.** 수평(선)
Something that is horizontal is flat and level with the ground, rather than at an angle to it.

wimp 복습
[wimp]

n. 겁쟁이, 약골 (wimp out **idiom** 겁을 먹고 안 하다)
If you wimp out, you decide not to do something that you had intended to do because you are too frightened.

disgust 복습
[disgʌ́st]

n. 혐오감, 역겨움, 넌더리; **v.** 혐오감을 유발하다, 역겹게 만들다
Disgust is a feeling of very strong dislike or disapproval.

figure out 복습

idiom ~을 생각해내다; 계산하다
If you figure out a solution to a problem or the reason for something, you succeed in solving it or understanding it.

giggle 복습
[gigl]

v. 낄낄 웃다; **n.** 낄낄 웃음
If someone giggles, they laugh in a childlike way, because they are amused, nervous, or embarrassed.

nod 복습
[nad]

v. (고개를) 끄덕이다; **n.** (고개를) 끄덕임
If you nod, you move your head downward and upward to show agreement, understanding, or approval.

tense**
[tens]

v. 긴장시키다, 팽팽하게 하다; 긴장하다; **a.** 긴장한, 긴박한; 팽팽한
If your muscles tense, if you tense, or if you tense your muscles, your muscles become tight and stiff, often because you are anxious or frightened.

approach 복습
[əpróutʃ]

v. 접근하다, 다가오다 **n.** 접근, 가까움
When you approach something, you get closer to it.

hassle
[hæsl]

v. 재촉하다, 들볶다; **n.** 귀찮은[번거로운] 상황
If someone hassles you, they cause problems for you, often by repeatedly telling you or asking you to do something, in an annoying way.

watchdog
[wátʃdɔːg]

n. 감시인
A watchdog is a person or committee whose job is to make sure that companies do not act illegally or irresponsibly.

flip someone off 복습

idiom 손가락으로 욕을 하다
If you flip someone off, you raise your middle finger to them in a very rude sign.

sensitive**
[sénsitiv]

a. 민감한, 예민한; 감수성이 강한
If you are sensitive to other people's needs, problems, or feelings, you show understanding and awareness of them.

pretend 복습
[priténd]

a. 가짜의, 꾸민; **v.** ～인 체하다, 가장하다
Something that is pretend is imaginary or not real.

get a free ride

idiom 거저 얻다, 무임 승차하다
If you get a free ride, you have an advantage or a benefit from a situation without doing anything to deserve it.

lively*
[láivli]

a. 생기에 넘치는, 기운찬, 활발한
You can describe someone as lively when they behave in an enthusiastic and cheerful way.

gesture 복습
[dʒéstʃər]

v. (손 · 머리 · 얼굴 등으로) 가리키다, 몸짓을 하다; **n.** 몸짓
If you gesture, you use movements of your hands or head in order to tell someone something or draw their attention to something.

react 복습
[riǽkt]

v. 반응하다, 반응을 보이다
When you react to something that has happened to you, you behave in a particular way because of it.

lean 복습
[liːn]

v. ～에 기대다; 기울이다, (몸을) 숙이다
If you lean on or against someone or something, you rest against them so that they partly support your weight.

punish 복습
[pʌ́niʃ]

v. 벌하다, 응징하다, 처벌하다 (punishment **n.** 벌, 처벌)
To punish someone means to make them suffer in some way because they have done something wrong.

passenger**
[pǽsəndʒər]

n. 승객
A passenger in a vehicle such as a bus, boat, or plane is a person who is travelling in it, but who is not driving it or working on it.

crowd***
[kraud]

n. 군중, 인파; **v.** 군집하다, 붐비다
A crowd is a large group of people who have gathered together, for example to watch or listen to something interesting, or to protest about something.

topple 복습
[tapl]

v. 넘어지다; 넘어뜨리다
If someone or something topples somewhere or if you topple them, they become unsteady or unstable and fall over.

scramble*
[skræmbl]

v. 기어오르다; 서로 (다투어) 빼앗다; 뒤섞다; **n.** 기어오르기
If you scramble over rocks or up a hill, you move quickly over them or up it using your hands to help you.

bounce 복습
[bauns]

v. 튀다, 튀게 하다; 급히 움직이다, 뛰어다니다; **n.** 튐, 바운드
If something bounces off a surface or is bounced off it, it reaches the surface and is reflected back.

flash 복습
[flæʃ]

v. (잠깐) 비치다, 번쩍이다; 비추다; (분노 등으로) 발끈[폭발]하다 **n.** 섬광, 번쩍임
If a light flashes or if you flash a light, it shines with a sudden bright light, especially as quick, regular flashes of light.

embarrass 복습
[imbǽrəs]

v. 당황스럽게 만들다 (embarrassing **a.** 난처한, 쑥스러운))
If something or someone embarrasses you, they make you feel shy or ashamed.

poet**
[póuit]

n. 시인
A poet is a person who writes poems.

scurry
[skə́:ri]

v. 종종걸음으로 달리다, 급히 가다
When people or small animals scurry somewhere, they move there quickly and hurriedly, especially because they are frightened.

instant 복습
[ínstənt]

a. 즉시의, 즉각적인; **n.** 즉시, 순간 (instantly **ad.** 즉시, 순간에)
You use instant to describe something that happens immediately.

blush 복습
[blʌʃ]

v. 얼굴을 붉히다, 얼굴이 빨개지다; **n.** (당황하거나 수치스러워) 얼굴이 붉어짐
When you blush, your face becomes redder than usual because you are ashamed or embarrassed.

hardly 복습
[há:rdli]

ad. 거의 ∼아니다, 전혀 ∼않다
When you say you can hardly do something, you are emphasizing that it is very difficult for you to do it.

take someone aback

idiom ∼를 깜짝 놀라게 하다
If you are taken aback by something, you are surprised or shocked by it and you cannot respond at once.

defensive*
[difénsiv]

a. 방어적인, 방어의, 수비의 (defensiveness **n.** 방어적임, 방어적)
Someone who is defensive is behaving in a way that shows they feel unsure or threatened.

stretch 복습
[stretʃ]

v. 기지개를 켜다; (팔 · 다리의 근육을) 당기다; 늘이다; 늘어지다; **n.** 기지개 켜기
When you stretch, you put your arms or legs out straight and tighten your muscles.

untie
[ʌntái]

v. 풀다, 끄르다; 자유롭게 하다
If you untie something such as string or rope, you undo it so that there is no knot or so that it is no longer tying something.

v. (금속 등이) 녹슬다, 부식하다; **n.** 녹 (rusty **a.** 녹슨)
If metal rusts or something rusts it, it becomes covered with rust.

mansion *
[mǽnʃən]

n. (인상적인) 대저택
A mansion is a very large house.

1분에 몇 단어를 읽는지 리딩 속도를 측정해보세요.

$$\frac{1{,}372 \text{ words}}{\text{reading time (\quad) sec}} \times 60 = (\quad) \text{ WPM}$$

Build Your Vocabulary

creak
[kri:k]

v. 삐걱거리다; **n.** 삐걱거리는 소리
If something creaks, it makes a short, high-pitched sound when it moves.

path^{복습}
[pæθ]

n. 길, 방향; 작은 길
A path is a long strip of ground which people walk along to get from one place to another.

trample^{복습}
[træmpl]

v. 짓밟다, 밟아 뭉개다, 무시하다; **n.** 쿵쿵거리며 걸음, 짓밟음
If someone tramples something or tramples on it, they step heavily and carelessly on it and damage it.

plant***
[plænt]

v. (나무 · 씨앗 등을) 심다; **n.** 식물, 초목 (replant **v.** 옮겨 심다)
When you plant a seed, plant, or young tree, you put it into the ground so that it will grow there.

stuck^{복습}
[stʌk]

a. 꽉 끼인, 움직일 수 없는; ~을 떨쳐버리지 못하는
If something is stuck in a particular position, it is fixed tightly in this position and is unable to move.

porch^{복습}
[pɔ:rtʃ]

n. (건물 입구에 지붕이 얹혀 있고 벽이 둘러진) 현관
A porch is a sheltered area at the entrance to a building, which has a roof and sometimes has walls.

teeter
[tí:tər]

v. 흔들리다, 망설이다; 시소를 타다; **n.** 시소
If someone or something teeters, they shake in an unsteady way, and seem to be about to lose their balance and fall over.

slight**
[slait]

a. 근소한, 약간의 (slightly **ad.** 약간, 조금)
Something that is slight is very small in degree or quantity.

splinter
[splíntər]

v. 쪼개지다, 산산조각이 되다; 쪼개다, 찢다; **n.** 부서진 조각
If something splinters or is splintered, it breaks into thin, sharp pieces.

practically***
[prǽktikəli]

ad. 거의, ~이나 마찬가지; 실지로, 실질상
Practically means almost, but not completely or exactly.

tear^{복습}
[ter]

① **v.** (tore–torn) 찢다, 찢어지다; **n.** 찢음 ② **n.** 눈물
If you tear paper, cloth, or another material, or if it tears, you pull it into two pieces or you pull it so that a hole appears in it.

knock^{복습}
[nak]

v. (문을) 두드리다, 노크하다; 치다, 부수다 (knocker **n.** 문 두드리는 고리쇠)
If you knock on something such as a door or window, you hit it, usually several times, to attract someone's attention.

odd^{복습}
[ad]

a. 이상한, 특이한
If you describe someone or something as odd, you think that they are strange or unusual.

fist[*]
[fist]

n. (쥔) 주먹
Your hand is referred to as your fist when you have bent your fingers in towards the palm in order to hit someone, to make an angry gesture, or to hold something.

shrunken
[ʃrʌ́ŋkən]

a. (보기 싫게) 쪼그라든
Someone or something that is shrunken has become smaller than they used to be.

bang^{복습}
[bæŋ]

v. 쾅[탕]하고 치다; 쾅 하고 닫다; **n.** 쾅[쿵] (하는 소리)
If you bang on something or if you bang it, you hit it hard, making a loud noise.

beg^{복습}
[beg]

v. 간청하다, 애원하다; 구걸하다
If you beg someone to do something, you ask them very anxiously or eagerly to do it.

doorknob
[dɔ́:rnàb]

n. (문의) 손잡이
A doorknob is a round handle on a door.

peer^{복습}
[piər]

v. 응시하다, 자세히 보다 **n.** (나이 · 신분이 같거나 비슷한) 또래
Your peers are the people who are the same age as you or who have the same status as you

curse^{복습}
[kə:rs]

n. 저주; 욕(설), 악담; **v.** 욕(설)을 하다; 저주를 내리다
If you say that there is a curse on someone, you mean that there seems to be a supernatural power causing unpleasant things to happen to them.

in the first place

idiom 우선, 먼저
You say in the first place when you are talking about the beginning of a situation or about the situation as it was before a series of events.

make sense^{복습}

idiom 의미가 통하다, 말이 되다
If something makes sense, it has a meaning that you can easily understand.

click[*]
[klik]

n. 딸깍[찰깍]하는 소리; **v.** 딸깍 소리를 내다
A click is a short, sharp sound.

lean^{복습}
[li:n]

v. ～에 기대다; 기울이다, (몸을) 숙이다
If you lean on or against someone or something, you rest against them so that they partly support your weight.

cane^{복습}
[kein]

n. 지팡이
A cane is a long thin stick with a curved or round top which you can use to support yourself when you are walking.

run-down
[rʌ́n-dàun]

a. (건물 · 장소가) 황폐한; (사업 등이) 부진한, 쇠퇴한
A run-down building or area is in very poor condition.

lavish[*]
[lǽviʃ]

a. 사치스런, 호화스러운; v. 아낌없이 주다, 낭비하다 (lavishly **ad.** 호화스럽게)
If you describe something as lavish, you mean that it is very elaborate and impressive and a lot of money has been spent on it.

decorate[**]
[dékərèit]

v. 장식하다, 꾸미다 (decorated **a.** 장식된, 훌륭하게 꾸민)
If you decorate something, you make it more attractive by adding things to it.

oval[*]
[óuvəl]

a. 타원형의, 달걀 모양의; n. 타원체
Oval things have a shape that is like a circle but is wider in one direction than the other.

encase
[inkéis]

v. 싸다, (상자 등에) 넣다
If a person or an object is encased in something, they are completely covered or surrounded by it.

ornate
[ɔːrnéit]

a. 화려하게 장식한, 잘 꾸민
An ornate building, piece of furniture, or object is decorated with complicated patterns or shapes.

mocking
[mákiŋ]

a. 조롱하는 (mockingly **ad.** 조롱하듯이)
A mocking expression indicates that you think someone or something is stupid or inferior.

poet[복습]
[póuit]

n. 시인
A poet is a person who writes poems.

awe
[ɔː]

n. 경외감, 외경심; v. 온통 경외심을 갖게 하다
Awe is the feeling of respect and amazement that you have when you are faced with something wonderful and often rather frightening.

doubt[복습]
[daut]

n. 의심, 의혹, 의문; v. 확신하지 못하다, 의심하다
If you have doubt or doubts about something, you feel uncertain about it and do not know whether it is true or possible.

obvious[복습]
[ábviəs]

a. 명백한, 분명한 (obviously **ad.** 분명히, 명백하게)
If something is obvious, it is easy to see or understand.

widen[*]
[waidn]

v. 넓어지다; 넓히다
If you widen something or if it widens, it becomes greater in measurement from one side or edge to the other.

couch[복습]
[kautʃ]

n. 소파, 긴 의자
A couch is a long, comfortable seat for two or three people.

stare[복습]
[stɛər]

v. 빤히 쳐다보다, 응시하다; n. 빤히 쳐다보기, 응시
If you stare at someone or something, you look at them for a long time.

eerie
[íəri]

a. (eerier–eeriest) 괴상한, 으스스한
If you describe something as eerie, you mean that it seems strange and frightening, and makes you feel nervous.

texture[*]
[tékstʃər]

n. 감촉, 질감; 직물; 직조법, 짜임새; 조직, 구성, 구조
The texture of something is the way that it feels when you touch it, for example how smooth or rough it is.

chin ^{복습}
[tʃin]

n. 턱
Your chin is the part of your face that is below your mouth and above your neck.

scar [*]
[ska:r]

v. 마음의 상처를 남기다, 흉터를 남기다; **n.** 흉터
If an unpleasant physical or emotional experience scars you, it has a permanent effect on your mind.

ordinary ^{**}
[ɔ́:rdənèri]

a. 보통의, 평범한
Ordinary people or things are normal and not special or different in any way.

rim [*]
[rim]

n. (둥근 물건의) 가장자리, 테두리; **v.** 둘러싸다, 테를 두르다
The rim of a circular object is its outside edge.

birthmark
[bɔ́:rθmà:rk]

n. (날 때부터 몸에 있는) 점, 모반
A birthmark is a mark on someone's skin that has been there since they were born.

cheek ^{복습}
[tʃi:k]

n. 뺨, 볼
Your cheeks are the sides of your face below your eyes.

extend ^{복습}
[iksténd]

v. 넓어지다, 퍼지다; (손 · 발 등을) 뻗다, 늘이다
If an object extends from a surface or place, it sticks out from it.

dissolve [*]
[dizálv]

v. (고체가) 녹다, 용해되다; 녹이다, 용해시키다
If a substance dissolves in liquid or if you dissolve it, it becomes mixed with the liquid and disappears.

wrinkle [*]
[riŋkl]

v. ~에 주름살지게 하다, 구겨지다; **n.** 주름, 잔주름
When you wrinkle your nose or forehead, or when it wrinkles, you tighten the muscles in your face so that the skin folds.

stuff ^{복습}
[stʌf]

v. 채워 넣다, 속을 채우다; **n.** 것(들), 물건, 물질
(overstuffed **a.** 속을 두툼하게 채운)
If you stuff a container or space with something, you fill it with something or with a quantity of things until it is full.

partly ^{복습}
[pá:rtli]

ad. 부분적으로, 어느 정도
You use partly to indicate that something happens or exists to some extent, but not completely.

plead [*]
[pli:d]

v. 간청하다, 탄원하다; 변론하다, 변호하다
If you plead with someone to do something, you ask them in an intense, emotional way to do it.

dignified
[dígnəfàid]

a. 위엄 있는, 품위 있는
If you say that someone or something is dignified, you mean they are calm, impressive and deserve respect.

1분에 몇 단어를 읽는지 리딩 속도를 측정해보세요.

$$\frac{1{,}201 \text{ words}}{\text{reading time (}\qquad\text{) sec}} \times 60 = (\qquad) \text{ WPM}$$

Build Your Vocabulary

stow [stou]	**v.** (짐을) 실어 넣다, 채워 넣다 If you stow something somewhere, you carefully put it there until it is needed.
mop [map]	**v.** 자루걸레로 닦다, 청소하다; **n.** 자루걸레 If you mop a surface such as a floor, you clean it with a mop.
deck* [dek]	**n.** 갑판; (카드 패의) 한 벌 A deck on a vehicle such as a bus or ship is a lower or upper area of it.
swab [swab]	**v.** (물걸레 등으로) 닦다; (상처 소독 · 테스트용 세균 샘플 채취 등에 쓰는) 면봉 If you swab something, you clean it using a wet cloth or a tool called a mop.
dump^{복습} [dʌmp]	**v.** 쏟아 버리다, 내버리다, 아무렇게나 내려놓다; **n.** 쓰레기 더미 If you dump something somewhere, you put it or unload it there quickly and carelessly.
figure^{복습} [fígjər]	**v.** 생각하다, 판단하다; 계산하다; **n.** 모습, 인물; 숫자, 계산; 도형, 도표 If you figure that something is the case, you think or guess that it is the case.
offer^{복습} [ɔ́:fər]	**v.** 제의[제안]하다; 제공하다; **n.** 제공 If you offer something to someone, you ask them if they would like to have it or use it.
ass^{복습} [æs]	**n.** (속어) 엉덩이 Your ass is your bottom.
get rid of^{복습}	**idiom** ~을 없애다, 제거하다, 처리하다 If you get rid of somebody or something, you make yourself free of somebody or something that is annoying you or that you do not want or you throw something away.
cul-de-sac [kʌl-də-sǽk]	**n.** [프랑스어] 막다른 골목 A cul-de-sac is a short road which is closed off at one end.
block^{복습} [blak]	**n.** 구역, 블록; 사각형 덩어리; **v.** (지나가지 못하게) 막다, 차단하다 A block in a town is an area of land with streets on all its sides.
stuck^{복습} [stʌk]	**a.** 꽉 끼인, 움직일 수 없는; ~을 떨쳐 버리지 못하는 If something is stuck in a particular position, it is fixed tightly in this position and is unable to move.

114

intention[**]
[inténʃən]

n. 의사, 의도
An intention is an idea or plan of what you are going to do.

break in

idiom (건물에) 침입하다
If you break in, you enter a building illegally or by force.

hop[복습]
[hap]

v. 깡충 뛰다, 뛰어오르다; **n.** 깡충깡충 뜀
If you hop, you move along by jumping.

might as well[복습]

idiom ～하는 편이 낫다
If you say that you might as well do something, or that you may as well do it, you mean that you will do it although you do not have a strong desire to do it and may even feel slightly unwilling to do it.

trample[복습]
[træmpl]

v. 짓밟다, 밟아 뭉개다, 무시하다; **n.** 쿵쿵거리며 걸음, 짓밟음
If someone tramples something or tramples on it, they step heavily and carelessly on it and damage it.

kill time

idiom (두어 시간 등의) 시간을 죽이다
If you are killing time, you are doing something because you have some time available, not because you really want to do it.

complicated[복습]
[kámplikèitid]

a. 복잡한
If you say that something is complicated, you mean it has so many parts or aspects that it is difficult to understand or deal with.

foul[복습]
[faul]

n. 파울, 반칙; **v.** 반칙을 범하다; **a.** (냄새가) 더러운, 악취 나는
A foul is an act in a game or sport that is not allowed according to the rules.

stoop[*]
[stu:p]

n. 현관 입구의 계단; **v.** 몸을 굽히다; (자세가) 구부정하다
A stoop is a small platform at the door of a building, with steps leading up to it.

casual[복습]
[kǽʒuəl]

a. 태평스러운, 무심한; 격식을 차리지 않는, 평상시의 (casually **ad.** 무심코)
If you are casual, you are, or you pretend to be, relaxed and not very concerned about what is happening or what you are doing.

tug[*]
[tʌg]

v. (세게) 당기다, 끌다; 노력[분투]하다; **n.** 힘껏 당김; 분투, 노력
If you tug something or tug at it, you give it a quick and usually strong pull.

untie[복습]
[ʌntái]

v. 풀다, 끄르다; 자유롭게 하다
If you untie something such as string or rope, you undo it so that there is no knot or so that it is no longer tying something.

drawstring[복습]
[drɔ́:striŋ]

n. (가방 · 바지 등을) 졸라매는 끈
A drawstring is a cord that goes through an opening, for example at the top of a bag or a pair of trousers.

grab[복습]
[græb]

v. 붙잡다, 움켜잡다; **n.** 움켜잡으려고 함
If you grab something, you take it or pick it up suddenly and roughly.

traction
[trǽkʃən]

n. 끌기, 견인력
Traction is a particular form of power that makes a vehicle move.

bother ^{복습}
[báðər]

v. 신경 쓰다, 애를 쓰다; 귀찮게 하다, 귀찮게 말을 걸다; n. 성가심

If you do not bother to do something or if you do not bother with it, you do not do it, consider it, or use it because you think it is unnecessary or because you are too lazy.

scornful ^{복습}
[skɔ́:rnfəl]

a. 경멸하는, 멸시하는 (scornfully ad. 경멸적으로, 깔보고)

If you are scornful of someone or something, you show contempt for them.

compliment [*]
[kámpləmənt]

v. 경의를 표하다, 칭찬하다; n. 찬사, 칭찬의 말

If you compliment someone, you praise or express admiration to them.

warn ^{복습}
[wɔ:rn]

v. 경고하다, 주의를 주다, 조심하라고 하다

If you warn someone about something such as a possible danger or problem, you tell them about it so that they are aware of it.

fist ^{복습}
[fist]

n. (쥔) 주먹

Your hand is referred to as your fist when you have bent your fingers in towards the palm in order to hit someone, to make an angry gesture, or to hold something.

beat ^{복습}
[bi:t]

v. 때리다, 두드리다; (게임 · 시합에서) 이기다; (심장이) 고동치다; n. 고동, 맥박

If you beat someone or something, you hit them very hard.

glare ^{복습}
[glɛər]

v. 노려보다; 번쩍번쩍 빛나다; n. 섬광; 노려봄

If you glare at someone, you look at them with an angry expression on your face.

sigh ^{복습}
[sai]

v. 한숨 쉬다; n. 한숨, 탄식

When you sigh, you let out a deep breath, as a way of expressing feelings such as disappointment, tiredness, or pleasure.

disgust ^{복습}
[disgʌ́st]

v. 혐오감을 유발하다, 역겹게 만들다; n. 혐오감, 역겨움, 넌더리

To disgust someone means to make them feel a strong sense of dislike and disapproval.

contempt [*]
[kəntémpt]

n. 경멸, 모욕

If you have contempt for someone or something, you have no respect for them or think that they are unimportant.

mess with

idiom ~을 방해하다

If you mess with someone, you treat them in a bad, rude, or annoying way, or to start an argument with them.

bet ^{복습}
[bet]

v. (~이) 틀림없다; (경마 · 내기 등에) 돈을 걸다; n. 내기; 내기 돈

You use expressions such as 'I bet,' 'I'll bet,' and 'you can bet' to indicate that you are sure something is true.

sack ^{복습}
[sæk]

n. 부대, 자루; (쇼핑 물건을 담는 크고 튼튼한 종이) 봉지

A sack is a large bag made of rough woven material.

pissant ^{복습}
[písæ̀nt]

n. 무가치한 것[사람]

A pissant is an insignificant or contemptible person.

stride [*]
[straid]

v. (strode–stridden) 성큼성큼 걷다; n. 큰 걸음, 활보

If you stride somewhere, you walk there with quick, long steps.

116

1. What did Larry confess to David over the phone?
   A. He was also cursed.
   B. He actually like Tori.
   C. He lived in Japan after living in Venezuela.
   D. He had never lived outside the US.

2. What did Tori say she did when David's pants fell down?
   A. She blushed.
   B. She sneezed.
   C. She closed her eyes.
   D. She turned around.

3. Why did Tori say that it was lucky David hadn't drank the lemonade?
   A. It might have been poison.
   B. It might have been face juice.
   C. He might have spilled it on himself.
   D. He might have gotten sick.

4. What part of the conversation about Mrs. Bayfield did Tori seem genuinely surprised about?
   A. The part about Mrs. Bayfield's cane had been stolen
   B. The part about David gave her the finger and pushed her over
   C. The part about David went back to Mrs. Bayfield's house
   D. The part about bringing the cane back to remove the curse

5. How did Ricky react to Tori?
    A. He called her a stooge.
    B. He said she smelled like tea.
    C. He accepted the tea and smiled.
    D. He ignored her completely.

6. Why did Ricky come along with David and his friends to Roger's house?
    A. Ricky wanted to watch his brother fight.
    B. Ricky wanted another shot at Glen.
    C. Ricky wanted to help his brother.
    D. Ricky wanted exercise.

7. What did Tori do during the fight?
    A. She just watched.
    B. She told them to stop fighting.
    C. She ran away to get the police.
    D. She got the cane back from Randy.

1분에 몇 단어를 읽는지 리딩 속도를 측정해보세요.

$$\frac{810 \text{ words}}{\text{reading time (} \quad \text{) sec}} \times 60 = (\quad) \text{ WPM}$$

Build Your Vocabulary

strike 복습
[straik]

v. (struck–stricken/struck) 발생하다, 덮치다; 갑자기 떠오르다; 치다, 부딪치다;
n. 파업; 공격, 공습
If something such as an illness or disaster strikes, it suddenly happens.

sarcastic 복습
[sa:rkǽstik]

a. 빈정대는, 비꼬는, 풍자적인 (sarcastically **ad.** 비꼬는 투로, 풍자적으로)
Someone who is sarcastic says or does the opposite of what they really mean in order to mock or insult someone.

definite 복습
[défənit]

a. 확실한, 확고한; 분명한, 뚜렷한 (definitely **ad.** 확실히, 명확히)
If something such as a decision or an arrangement is definite, it is firm and clear, and unlikely to be changed.

gasp *
[gǽsp]

n. (숨이 막히는 듯) 헉 하는 소리를 냄; **v.** 숨이 턱 막히다, 헉 하고 숨을 쉬다
A gasp is a short quick breath of air that you take in through your mouth, especially when you are surprised, shocked, or in pain.

stuff 복습
[stʌf]

n. 것(들), 물건, 물질; **v.** 채워 넣다, 속을 채우다
You can use stuff to refer to things such as a substance, a collection of things, events, or ideas, or the contents of something in a general way without mentioning the thing itself by name.

sink 복습
[siŋk]

v. 가라앉다, 빠지다; **n.** (부엌의) 싱크대, 개수대 (sinking **a.** 가라앉는)
If you have a sinking feeling, you suddenly become depressed or lose hope.

slacks
[slæks]

n. (정장용이 아닌) 바지
Slacks are casual trousers.

sigh 복습
[sai]

v. 한숨 쉬다; **n.** 한숨, 탄식
When you sigh, you let out a deep breath, as a way of expressing feelings such as disappointment, tiredness, or pleasure.

apologize 복습
[əpálədʒàiz]

v. 사과하다, 사죄하다
When you apologize to someone, you say that you are sorry that you have hurt them or caused trouble for them.

get a free ride 복습

idiom 거저 얻다, 무임 승차하다
If you get a free ride, you have an advantage or a benefit from a situation without doing anything to deserve it.

snap 복습
[snæp]

v. (화난 목소리로) 딱딱거리다; 딱[툭] (하고) 부러뜨리다; **n.** 찰칵 하는 소리
If someone snaps at you, they speak to you in a sharp, unfriendly way.

leech
[li:tʃ]

n. [동물] 거머리
A leech is a small animal which looks like a worm and lives in water. Leeches feed by attaching themselves to other animals and sucking their blood.

slam^{복습}
[slæm]

v. 세게 놓다; 쾅[탁] 닫다
If you slam something down, you put it there quickly and with great force.

gnaw
[nɔ:]

v. 갉아먹다, 물어뜯다, 괴롭히다
If a feeling or thought gnaws at you, it causes you to keep worrying.

snot^{복습}
[snat]

n. 콧물; 버릇없는 사람
Snot is the substance that is produced inside your nose.

suggest^{복습}
[səgdʒést]

v. 암시하다; 제안하다 (suggestion **n.** 제안; 제시)
If you suggest something, you put forward a plan or idea for someone to think about.

dare^{복습}
[dɛər]

v. 감히 ~하다, 무릅쓰다, 도전하다
If you dare to do something, you do something which requires a lot of courage.

hopeless[*]
[hóuplis]

a. 가망 없는, 절망적인
Someone or something thing that is hopeless is certain to fail or be unsuccessful.

1분에 몇 단어를 읽는지 리딩 속도를 측정해보세요.

$$\frac{1{,}649 \text{ words}}{\text{reading time (} \qquad \text{) sec}} \times 60 = (\qquad) \text{ WPM}$$

Build Your Vocabulary

anxious 복습
[金ŋkʃəs]

a. 걱정하는, 염려하는; 열망하는, 간절히 바라는 (anxiously **ad.** 걱정스럽게)
If you are anxious to do something or anxious that something should happen, you very much want to do it or very much want it to happen.

stare 복습
[stɛər]

v. 빤히 쳐다보다, 응시하다; **n.** 빤히 쳐다보기, 응시
If you stare at someone or something, you look at them for a long time.

cabinet *
[kǽbənit]

n. 캐비닛, 보관장
A cabinet is a cupboard used for storing things such as medicine or alcoholic drinks or for displaying decorative things in.

counter 복습
[káuntər]

n. (부엌의) 조리대; 계산대; **v.** 반박하다
A counter is a flat surface in a kitchen which is easy to clean and on which you can prepare food.

sip *
[sip]

v. 찔끔찔끔 마시다; **n.** 한 모금
If you sip a drink or sip at it, you drink by taking just a small amount at a time.

flash 복습
[flæʃ]

v. (잠깐) 비치다, 번쩍이다; 비추다; (분노 등으로) 발끈[폭발]하다 **n.** 섬광, 번쩍임
If a light flashes or if you flash a light, it shines with a sudden bright light, especially as quick, regular flashes of light.

fourscore 복습
[fɔːrskɔːr]

a. 80의, 20의 4배의
Fourscore means four times twenty.

swallow 복습
[swálou]

v. 삼키다, 목구멍으로 넘기다; (초조해서) 마른침을 삼키다
If you swallow something, you cause it to go from your mouth down into your stomach.

witch 복습
[witʃ]

n. 마녀
In fairy stories, a witch is a woman, usually an old woman, who has evil magic powers.

widen 복습
[waidn]

v. 넓어지다; 넓히다
If you widen something or if it widens, it becomes greater in measurement from one side or edge to the other.

curse 복습
[kəːrs]

n. 저주; 욕(설), 악담; **v.** 욕(설)을 하다; 저주를 내리다
If you say that there is a curse on someone, you mean that there seems to be a supernatural power causing unpleasant things to happen to them.

in a way	**idiom** 어느 정도는, 어떤 면에서는 If you say that something is true in a way, you mean that although it is not completely true, it is true to a limited extent or in certain respects.
hang out ^{복습}	**idiom** 사귀다, 어울리다 If you hang out, you spend a lot of time in a place or with a person or a group of people.
redden ^{복습} [redn]	**v.** 빨개지다, 붉어지다 If someone reddens or their face reddens, their face turns pink or red, often because they are embarrassed or angry.
occur ^{복습} [əkə́:r]	**v.** 생각이 떠오르다; 일어나다, 생기다 If a thought or idea occurs to you, you suddenly think of it or realize it.
eyebrow[*] [áibràu]	**n.** 눈썹 Your eyebrows are the lines of hair which grow above your eyes.
knock ^{복습} [nak]	**v.** 치다, 부수다; (문을) 두드리다, 노크하다 If you knock something, you touch or hit it roughly, especially so that it falls or moves.
cane ^{복습} [kein]	**n.** 지팡이 A cane is a long thin stick with a curved or round top which you can use to support yourself when you are walking.
give someone the finger [bird] ^{복습}	**idiom** 가운데 손가락을 들어 보이며 모욕하다 If you give someone the finger, you make a rude sign at them with your middle finger.
shrug ^{복습} [ʃrʌg]	**v.** (양 손바닥을 내보이면서 어깨를) 으쓱하다; **n.** (어깨를) 으쓱하기 If you shrug, you raise your shoulders to show that you are not interested in something or that you do not know or care about something.
whisper ^{복습} [hwíspər]	**v.** 속삭이다 When you whisper, you say something very quietly.
nod ^{복습} [nad]	**v.** (고개를) 끄덕이다; **n.** (고개를) 끄덕임 If you nod, you move your head downward and upward to show agreement, understanding, or approval.
pitcher ^{복습} [pítʃər]	① **n.** 물 주전자 ② **n.** 투수, 피처 A pitcher is a jug.
conclusive [kənklú:siv]	**a.** 결정적인, 확실한 (conclusively **ad.** 단정적으로) Conclusive evidence shows that something is certainly true.
preserve ^{복습} [prizə́:rv]	**v.** 보존하다, 유지하다 If you preserve something, you take action to save it or protect it from damage or decay.
exclaim ^{복습} [ikskléim]	**v.** 외치다, 소리치다 If you exclaim, you say or shout something suddenly because of surprise, fear and pleasure.

remind ^{복습}
[rimáind]

v. 생각나게 하다, 상기시키다, 일깨우다
If someone reminds you of a fact or event that you already know about, they say something which makes you think about it.

poet ^{복습}
[póuit]

n. 시인
A poet is a person who writes poems.

blush ^{복습}
[blʌʃ]

v. 얼굴을 붉히다, 얼굴이 빨개지다; **n.** (당황하거나 수치스러워) 얼굴이 붉어짐
When you blush, your face becomes redder than usual because you are ashamed or embarrassed.

beg ^{복습}
[beg]

v. 간청하다, 애원하다; 구걸하다
If you beg someone to do something, you ask them very anxiously or eagerly to do it.

suspicious ^{복습}
[səspíʃəs]

a. 의심하는, 수상쩍은 (suspiciously **ad.** 의심하듯이, 수상쩍게)
If you are suspicious of someone or something, you do not trust them, and are careful when dealing with them.

glance ^{복습}
[glæns]

v. 흘긋 보다, 잠깐 보다; **n.** 흘긋 봄
If you glance at something or someone, you look at them very quickly and then look away again immediately.

genuine *
[dʒénjuin]

a. 진심의, 참된; 진짜의, 진품의 (genuinely **ad.** 진정으로)
Genuine refers to things such as emotions that are real and not pretended.

out of the corner of one's eye

idiom 곁눈질로
If you see something out of the corner of your eye, you see it not very clearly because you see it from the side of your eye and are not looking straight at it.

make a crack

idiom 놀리다
If you make a crack, you tell a slightly rude or cruel joke.

greet ^{복습}
[gri:t]

v. 맞다, 환영하다
When you greet someone, you say 'Hello' or shake hands with them.

make a face

idiom 얼굴을 찌푸리다
If you make a face, you twist your face to indicate a certain mental or emotional state.

obvious ^{복습}
[ábviəs]

a. 명백한, 분명한 (obviously **ad.** 분명히, 명백하게)
If something is obvious, it is easy to see or understand.

pinky ^{복습}
[píŋki]

n. (= pinkie) 새끼손가락
Your pinky is the smallest finger on your hand.

dainty
[déinti]

a. 조심스러운, 얌전한; 앙증맞은 (daintily **ad.** 우아하게, 섬세하게)
If you describe a movement, person, or object as dainty, you mean that they are small, delicate, and pretty.

reluctant *
[rilʌ́ktənt]

a. 꺼리는, 마지못해 하는, 주저하는 (reluctantly **ad.** 마지못해서, 꺼려하며)
If you are reluctant to do something, you are unwilling to do it and hesitate before doing it, or do it slowly and without enthusiasm.

124

leash
[li:ʃ]

n. 가죽 끈, 사슬; 속박, 통제
A dog's leash is a long thin piece of leather or a chain, which you attach to the dog's collar so that you can keep the dog under control.

quizzical
[kwízikəl]

a. 미심쩍어하는; 기묘한, 우스꽝스러운 (quizzically ad. 미심쩍게)
If you give someone a quizzical look or smile, you look at them in a way that shows that you are surprised or amused by their behavior.

thumb^{복습}
[θʌm]

n. 엄지손가락; v. (책을) 엄지손가락으로 넘기다
Your thumb is the short thick part on the side of your hand next to your four fingers.

pound^{복습}
[paund]

① v. 쿵쿵 울리다, 마구 치다, 세게 두드리다; n. 타격 ② n. 파운드(무게의 단위)
③ n. 주인 잃은 개 보호소
A pound is a place where dogs and cats found wandering in the street are taken and kept until they are claimed by their owners.

kneel[*]
[ni:l]

v. 무릎 꿇다
When you kneel, you bend your legs so that your knees are touching the ground.

rub^{복습}
[rʌb]

v. 비비다, 문지르다; 스치다; n. 문지르기
If you rub a part of your body, you move your hand or fingers backwards and forwards over it while pressing firmly.

execute[*]
[éksikjù:t]

v. 처형하다; 실행하다, 집행하다
To execute someone means to kill them as a punishment for a serious crime.

lick[*]
[lik]

v. 핥다; n. 한 번 핥기, 핥아먹기
When people or animals lick something, they move their tongue across its surface.

might as well^{복습}

idiom ~하는 편이 낫다
If you say that you might as well do something, or that you may as well do it, you mean that you will do it although you do not have a strong desire to do it and may even feel slightly unwilling to do it.

adjust^{복습}
[ədʒʌ́st]

v. (옷매무새 등을) 바로 하다; 조절하다, 조정하다
If you adjust something such as your clothing or a machine, you correct or alter its position or setting.

declare^{복습}
[diklɛ́ər]

v. 선언하다; 단언하다
If you declare something, you state officially and formally that it exists or is the case.

1분에 몇 단어를 읽는지 리딩 속도를 측정해보세요

$$\frac{1{,}829 \text{ words}}{\text{reading time (} \qquad \text{) sec}} \times 60 = (\qquad) \text{ WPM}$$

Build Your Vocabulary

sidewalk 복습
[sáidwɔ:k]

n. (포장한) 보도, 인도
A sidewalk is a path with a hard surface by the side of a road.

dropping
[drápiŋ]

n. (pl.) (새나 작은 동물의) 똥; 낙하, 투하
Droppings are the feces of birds and small animals.

bush 복습
[buʃ]

n. 관목, 덤불
A bush is a large plant which is smaller than a tree and has a lot of branches.

tense 복습
[tens]

v. 긴장시키다, 팽팽하게 하다; 긴장하다; **a.** 긴장한, 긴박한; 팽팽한
If your muscles tense, if you tense, or if you tense your muscles, your muscles become tight and stiff, often because you are anxious or frightened.

upbeat
[ʌ́pbì:t]

a. 긍정적인, 낙관적인
If people or their opinions are upbeat, they are cheerful and hopeful about a situation.

enthusiastic*
[inθù:ziǽstik]

a. 열렬한, 열광적인
If you are enthusiastic about something, you show how much you like or enjoy it by the way that you behave and talk.

pee
[pi:]

v. 오줌을 누다; **n.** 오줌 (누기)
When someone pees, they urinate.

tag along 복습

idiom (청하거나 초대하지 않는데도) (~를) 따라가다
If you tag along, you go somewhere with someone, especially when you have not been invited.

cul-de-sac 복습
[kʌl-də-sæk]

n. [프랑스어] 막다른 골목
A cul-de-sac is a short road which is closed off at one end.

fist 복습
[fist]

n. (쥔) 주먹
Your hand is referred to as your fist when you have bent your fingers in towards the palm in order to hit someone, to make an angry gesture, or to hold something.

curly 복습
[kə́:rli]

a. 곱슬곱슬한
Curly hair is full of curls.

fly 복습
[flai]

n. (바지 앞의) 지퍼[단추]로 잠그는 부분; 파리; **v.** (새·곤충이) 날다
The front opening on a pair of trousers is referred to as the fly. It usually consists of a zip or row of buttons behind a band of cloth.

quiver ^{복습}
[kwívər]

v. 떨다, 떨리다; n. (감정 · 몸의 일부가) 떨림
If something quivers, it shakes with very small movements.

whine ^{복습}
[hwain]

v. 징징거리다, 우는 소리를 하다 (whiny **a.** 불평하는, 투덜대는)
If something or someone whines, they make a long, high-pitched noise, especially one which sounds sad or unpleasant.

mocking ^{복습}
[mákiŋ]

a. 조롱하는 (mockingly **ad.** 조롱하듯이, 희롱하여)
A mocking expression indicates that you think someone or something is stupid or inferior.

glare ^{복습}
[glɛər]

v. 노려보다; 번쩍번쩍 빛나다; n. 섬광; 노려봄
If you glare at someone, you look at them with an angry expression on your face.

ass ^{복습}
[æs]

n. (속어) 엉덩이
Your ass is your bottom.

gag ^{복습}
[gæg]

① v. 말문을 막다, 재갈을 물리다; n. 재갈 ② n. 익살, 개그; v. 농담하다
If someone gags you, they tie a piece of cloth around your mouth in order to stop you from speaking or shouting.

scornful ^{복습}
[skɔ́:rnfəl]

a. 경멸하는, 멸시하는 (scornfully **ad.** 경멸적으로, 깔보고)
If you are scornful of someone or something, you show contempt for them.

challenge **
[ʧǽlindʒ]

v. (경쟁 · 싸움 등을) 걸다; 도전하다; n. 도전
If you challenge someone, you invite them to fight or compete with you in some way.

throughout **
[θru:áut]

prep. ～동안 죽, 내내; 도처에
If you say that something happens throughout a particular period of time, you mean that it happens during the whole of that period.

sleepless
[slí:plis]

a. 잠을 못 자는, 불면의; 잠을 못 이루는
A sleepless night is one during which you do not sleep.

occur ^{복습}
[əkɔ́:r]

v. 생각이 떠오르다; 일어나다, 생기다
If a thought or idea occurs to you, you suddenly think of it or realize it.

flip someone off ^{복습}

idiom 손가락으로 욕을 하다
If you flip someone off, you raise your middle finger to them in a very rude sign.

warn ^{복습}
[wɔ:rn]

v. 경고하다, 주의를 주다, 조심하라고 하다
If you warn someone about something such as a possible danger or problem, you tell them about it so that they are aware of it.

stoop ^{복습}
[stu:p]

n. 현관 입구의 계단; v. 몸을 굽히다; (자세가) 구부정하다
A stoop is a small platform at the door of a building, with steps leading up to it.

gang *
[gæŋ]

n. 패거리, 무리; 갱, 범죄 조직
A gang is a group of people who go around together and often deliberately cause trouble.

bang ^{복습}
[bæŋ]

v. 쾅[탕]하고 치다; 쾅 하고 닫다; n. 쾅[쿵] (하는 소리)
If you bang on something or if you bang it, you hit it hard, making a loud noise.

stumble *
[stʌmbl]

v. 비틀거리다, 휘청거리다; 발이 걸리다, 발을 헛디디다
If you stumble, you put your foot down awkwardly while you are walking or running and nearly fall over.

protect ^{복습}
[prətékt]

v. 보호하다, 막다, 지키다 (protection n. 보호)
To protect someone or something means to prevent them from being harmed or damaged.

smash ^{복습}
[smæʃ]

v. 박살내다, 부딪치다, 충돌하다; n. 강타; 박살내기
If you smash something or if it smashes, it breaks into many pieces, for example when it is hit or dropped.

slug
[slʌg]

v. ~을 세게 때리다
If you slug someone, you hit them hard.

grab ^{복습}
[græb]

v. 붙잡다, 움켜잡다; n. 움켜잡으려고 함
If you grab something, you take it or pick it up suddenly and roughly.

rip *
[rip]

v. 찢다, 벗겨내다; n. 찢어진 틈, 잡아 찢음
When something rips or when you rip it, you tear it forcefully with your hands or with a tool such as a knife.

dizzy *
[dízi]

a. 현기증 나는, 아찔한 (dizzily ad. 현기증 나게)
If you feel dizzy, you feel as if everything is spinning round and being unable to balance.

defend *
[difénd]

v. 방어하다, 지키다
If you defend someone or something, you take action in order to protect them.

fling **
[fliŋ]

v. (몸이나 신체 일부를 갑자기 힘껏) 던지다; 내던지다, 내팽개치다
If you fling yourself somewhere, you move or jump there suddenly and with a lot of force.

claw *
[klɔː]

v. (손톱 · 발톱으로) 할퀴다; n. (동물 · 새의) 발톱; (게 등의) 집게발
If an animal claws at something, it scratches or damages it with its claws.

slam ^{복습}
[slæm]

v. 세게[힘껏] 놓다; 쾅[탁] 닫다
If you slam something down, you put it there quickly and with great force.

charge ^{복습}
[tʃaːrdʒ]

v. 돌격하다, 돌진하다; 청구하다; 충전하다, 채우다; n. 요금; 책임
If you charge toward someone or something, you move quickly and aggressively toward them.

grip ^{복습}
[grip]

v. 꽉 잡다, 움켜잡다; n. 잡음, 움켜쥠; 손잡이
If you grip something, you take hold of it with your hand and continue to hold it firmly.

helpless ^{복습}
[hélplis]

a. 무력한, 속수무책의 (helplessly ad. 무력하게, 어쩔 수 없이)
If you are helpless, you do not have the strength or power to do anything useful or to control or protect yourself.

128

fluid *
[flu:id]

a. 유동성의, 불안정한; **n.** 유체(流體), 유동체
Something that is fluid is like a liquid.

jam **
[dʒæm]

v. (세게) 밀다, 밀어 넣다; 움직이지 못하게 되다; **n.** 잼; 혼잡, 교통 체증
If you jam something somewhere, you push or put it there roughly.

lap 복습
[læp]

n. 무릎; (경주에서 트랙의) 한 바퀴
If you have something on your lap, it is on top of your legs and near to your body.

duck **
[dʌk]

① **v.** 피하다, 머리를 홱 숙이다 ② **n.** 오리
If you duck, you move your head or the top half of your body quickly downward to avoid something that might hit you, or to avoid being seen.

lunge 복습
[lʌndʒ]

v. (사람을 공격하거나 무엇을 움켜잡으려고) 달려들다, 돌진하다; **n.** 돌진
If you lunge in a particular direction, you move in that direction suddenly and clumsily.

wince
[wins]

v. (아픔·무서움 때문에) 움찔하다, 주춤하다, 움츠리다; **n.** 위축
If you wince, you suddenly look as if you are suffering because you feel pain.

lick 복습
[lik]

v. 핥다; **n.** 한 번 핥기, 핥아먹기
When people or animals lick something, they move their tongue across its surface.

midair 복습
[midέər]

n. 공중, 중천
If something happens in midair, it happens in the air, rather than on the ground.

drag 복습
[dræg]

v. 끌다, 힘들게 움직이다; **n.** 견인, 끌기
If you drag something, you pull it along the ground.

bloody 복습
[blʌdi]

a. 피투성이의; 피비린내 나는, 유혈이 낭자한
You can describe someone or something as bloody if they are covered in a lot of blood.

pin **
[pin]

v. ~을 꼼짝 못하게 누르다; 핀으로 꽂다, 고정하다; **n.** 핀, 장식
If someone pins you to something, they press you against a surface so that you cannot move.

give up

idiom 포기하다, 단념하다
If you give up, you decide that you cannot do something and stop trying to do it.

groan *
[groun]

v. 신음하다, 끙끙거리다; **n.** 신음, 끙끙거리는 소리
If you groan, you make a long, low sound because you are in pain, or because you are upset or unhappy about something.

chin 복습
[tʃin]

n. 턱
Your chin is the part of your face that is below your mouth and above your neck.

stretch 복습
[stretʃ]

v. (팔·다리의 근육을) 당기다; 늘이다; 늘어지다; 기지개를 켜다; **n.** 기지개 켜기
When you stretch, you put your arms or legs out straight and tighten your muscles.

gasp ^{복습}
[gæsp]

v. 숨이 턱 막히다, 헉 하고 숨을 쉬다; n. (숨이 막히는 듯) 헉 하는 소리를 냄
When you gasp, you take a short quick breath through your mouth, especially when you are surprised, shocked, or in pain.

cough ^{복습}
[kɔːf]

v. 기침하다; n. (헛)기침
When you cough, you force air out of your throat with a sudden, harsh noise.

moan[*]
[moun]

v. 신음하다; 투덜거리다, 불평하다; n. 신음 (소리)
If you moan, you make a low sound, usually because you are unhappy or in pain.

spit[*]
[spit]

v. (spat–spat) (입에 든 음식 등을) 뱉다; 침을 뱉다; n. 침
If you spit liquid or food somewhere, you force a small amount of it out of your mouth.

sleeve ^{복습}
[sliːv]

n. (옷의) 소매, 소맷자락
The sleeves of a coat, shirt, or other item of clothing are the parts that cover your arms.

beam ^{복습}
[biːm]

v. 활짝 웃다; n. 빛줄기
If you say that someone is beaming, you mean that they have a big smile on their face because they are happy, pleased, or proud about something.

slip ^{복습}
[slip]

v. (재빨리 · 슬며시) 놓다; (어떤 위치 · 손을 벗어나) 미끄러지다, 빠져 나가다; n. (작은 종이) 조각, 쪽지
If you slip something somewhere, you put it there quickly in a way that does not attract attention.

throb[*]
[θrab]

v. 욱신거리다; (심장이) 고동치다, 맥이 뛰다; n. 고동, 맥박
If part of your body throbs, you feel a series of strong and usually painful beats there.

nod ^{복습}
[nad]

v. (고개를) 끄덕이다; n. (고개를) 끄덕임
If you nod, you move your head downward and upward to show agreement, understanding, or approval.

declare ^{복습}
[diklέər]

v. 선언하다; 단언하다
If you declare something, you state officially and formally that it exists or is the case.

mess with ^{복습}

idiom ~을 방해하다
If you mess with someone, you treat them in a bad, rude, or annoying way, or to start an argument with them.

gut ^{복습}
[gʌt]

n. (사람의) 배; 소화관; (pl.) 배짱
You can refer to someone's stomach as their gut, especially when it is very large and sticks out.

stand up to ^{복습}

idiom (용감히) 맞서다
If you stand up to someone or something, you resist them or defend your position against them.

rotten ^{복습}
[ratn]

a. 썩은, 부패한; 형편없는, 끔찍한
If food, wood, or another substance is rotten, it has decayed and can no longer be used.

| **get the better of** ^{복습} | **idiom** ~을 이기다, 능가하다
If you get the better of someone, you defeat them in a contest, fight, or argument. |

get the better of ^{복습}

idiom ~을 이기다, 능가하다
If you get the better of someone, you defeat them in a contest, fight, or argument.

limp ^{복습}
[limp]

v. 다리를 절다, 절뚝거리다; **a.** 기운이 없는, 축 처진
If a person or animal limps, they walk with difficulty or in an uneven way because one of their legs or feet is hurt.

pick on

idiom (부당하게) ~을 괴롭히다; ~을 선택하다
If you pick on someone, you treat them badly or unfairly, especially repeatedly.

triumphant
[traiʌ́mfənt]

a. 크게 성공한, 큰 승리를 거둔 (triumphantly **ad.** 의기양양하여)
Someone who is triumphant has gained a victory or succeeded in something and feels very happy about it.

chop ^{복습}
[tʃap]

v. 내려치다; (음식 재료를 토막으로) 썰다; **n.** 토막; 내리치기
If you chop, you make a short quick downward stroke.

trace ^{복습}
[treis]

n. 자취, 흔적; 극미량, 조금; **v.** 추적하다, (추적하여) 찾아내다
A trace is a sign which shows you that someone or something has been in a place.

1분에 몇 단어를 읽는지 리딩 속도를 측정해보세요.

$$\frac{1{,}003 \text{ words}}{\text{reading time (} \quad \text{) sec}} \times 60 = (\quad\quad) \text{ WPM}$$

Build Your Vocabulary

spot^{복습}
[spat]

n. 장소, 지점; 반점, 얼룩; **v.** 발견하다, 분별하다
You can refer to a particular place as a spot.

make up for^{복습}

idiom ~에 대해 보상하다. (잘못된 상황을 바로잡을 수 있도록) 만회하다
If you make up for something, you do something good for someone because you have treated them badly or because they have done something good for you.

awesome
[ɔ́:səm]

a. 굉장한, 아주 멋진; 무시무시한
An awesome person or thing is very impressive and often frightening.

responsibility^{복습}
[rispɑ̀nsəbíləti]

n. 책임(감), 책무
If you have responsibility for something or someone, or if they are your responsibility, it is your job or duty to deal with them and to take decisions relating to them.

discipline^{**}
[dísəplin]

n. 규율, 훈련; **v.** 훈련하다 (self–discipline **n.** 자기 훈련)
Discipline is the practice of making people obey rules or standards of behavior, and punishing them when they do not.

brush^{**}
[brʌʃ]

v. ~을 스치다; 솔질을 하다; **n.** 붓, 솔
If one thing brushes against another or if you brush one thing against another, the first thing touches the second thing lightly while passing it.

pinky^{복습}
[píŋki]

n. (= pinkie) 새끼손가락
Your pinky is the smallest finger on your hand.

palm[*]
[pa:m]

① **n.** 손바닥 ② **n.** 종려나무, 야자나무
The palm of your hand is the inside part.

wiggle^{복습}
[wigl]

v. (좌우 · 상하로 짧게) 씰룩씰룩[꼼지락꼼지락] 움직이다
If you wiggle something or if it wiggles, it moves up and down or from side to side in small quick movements.

loosen[*]
[lu:sn]

v. 풀다, 느슨해지다
If you loosen your grip on something, or if your grip loosens, you hold it less tightly.

interlock
[intərlák]

v. 서로 맞물리다, 서로 겹치다
Things that interlock or are interlocked go between or through each other so that they are linked.

run-down ^{복습}
[rʌ́n-dàun]

a. (건물 · 장소가) 황폐한; (사업 등이) 부진한, 쇠퇴한
A run-down building or area is in very poor condition.

mansion ^{복습}
[mǽnʃən]

n. (인상적인) 대저택
A mansion is a very large house.

announce ^{복습}
[ənáuns]

v. 발표하다, 알리다
If you announce something, you tell people about it publicly or officially.

block ^{복습}
[blak]

v. (지나가지 못하게) 막다, 차단하다; **n.** 사각형 덩어리; 구역, 블록
If you block someone's way, you prevent them from going somewhere or entering a place by standing in front of them.

spooky
[spú:ki]

a. 유령(이 나올 것) 같은, 으스스한, 무시무시한
A place that is spooky has a frightening atmosphere, and makes you feel that there are ghosts around.

leash ^{복습}
[li:ʃ]

n. 가죽 끈, 사슬; 속박, 통제
A dog's leash is a long thin piece of leather or a chain, which you attach to the dog's collar so that you can keep the dog under control.

gesture ^{복습}
[dʒésʧər]

v. (손 · 머리 · 얼굴 등으로) 가리키다, 몸짓을 하다; **n.** 몸짓
If you gesture, you use movements of your hands or head in order to tell someone something or draw their attention to something.

mystical *
[místikəl]

a. 신령스러운, 신비로운
Something that is mystical involves spiritual powers and influences that most people do not understand.

squeeze *
[skwi:z]

v. 꽉 쥐다, 짜다, 압착하다; 쑤셔 넣다; **n.** 압착, 짜냄
If you squeeze something, you press it firmly, usually with your hands.

sweat ^{복습}
[swet]

v. 땀 흘리다; 습기가 차다; **n.** 땀 (sweaty **a.** 땀흘린, 땀범벅인)
When you sweat, drops of liquid comes through your skin.

approach ^{복습}
[əpróuʧ]

v. 접근하다, 다가오다 **n.** 접근, 가까움
When you approach something, you get closer to it.

rust ^{복습}
[rʌst]

v. (금속 등이) 녹슬다, 부식하다; **n.** 녹 (rusty **a.** 녹슨)
If metal rusts or something rusts it, it becomes covered with rust.

chill *
[ʧil]

n. 오싹한 느낌; 냉기, 한기
If something sends a chill through you, it gives you a sudden feeling of fear or anxiety.

spine
[spain]

n. 등뼈, 척추
Your spine is the row of bones down your back.

knock ^{복습}
[nak]

v. (문을) 두드리다, 노크하다; 치다, 부수다
If you knock on something such as a door or window, you hit it, usually several times, to attract someone's attention.

quizzical ^{복습}
[kwízikəl]

a. 미심쩍어하는; 기묘한, 우스꽝스러운 (quizzically **ad.** 미심쩍게)
If you give someone a quizzical look or smile, you look at them in a way that shows that you are surprised or amused by their behavior.

shrunken ^{복습}
[ʃrʌ́ŋkən]

a. (보기 싫게) 쪼그라든
Someone or something that is shrunken has become smaller than they used to be.

bang ^{복습}
[bæŋ]

v. 쾅 하고 닫다; 쾅[탕]하고 치다; **n.** 쾅[쿵] (하는 소리)
If you bang a door or if it bangs, it closes suddenly with a loud noise.

click ^{복습}
[klik]

v. 딸깍 소리를 내다; **n.** 딸깍[찰깍]하는 소리
If something clicks or if you click it, it makes a short, sharp sound.

peer ^{복습}
[piər]

v. 응시하다, 자세히 보다; **n.** (나이 · 신분이 같거나 비슷한) 또래
Your peers are the people who are the same age as you or who have the same status as you.

dart ^{복습}
[da:rt]

v. (시선 · 화살 · 빛 등을) 던지다, 쏘다; **n.** 던지는 화살, 다트
If you dart a look at someone or something, or if your eyes dart to them, you look at them very quickly.

stoop ^{복습}
[stu:p]

v. 몸을 굽히다; (자세가) 구부정하다; **n.** 현관 입구의 계단
If you stoop, you bend your body forwards and downwards.

stern *
[stə:rn]

a. 엄한, 단호한
Someone who is stern is very serious and strict.

warn ^{복습}
[wɔ:rn]

v. 경고하다, 주의를 주다, 조심하라고 하다 (warning **n.** 경고)
If you warn someone about something such as a possible danger or problem, you tell them about it so that they are aware of it.

1. What did Mrs. Bayfield make David do to break the curse even after returning the cane?
   A. She made him pay the bill for the broken window.
   B. She made him let her make a mask of his face.
   C. She made him drink from a glass and kiss Tori.
   D. She made him go bring Scott and the others back to her.

2. How did David know that Mrs. Bayfield and Tori knew each other?
   A. Mrs. Bayfield winked at David.
   B. Mrs. Bayfield called him Mr. Ballinger.
   C. Mrs. Bayfield and Tori both had green eyes.
   D. Mrs. Bayfield and Tori both had the same last name.

3. Why had David's name and phone number been written down near Mrs. Bayfield's phone?
   A. Mrs. Bayfield had written it to complain to his parents.
   B. Mrs. Bayfield had written it to demand an apology.
   C. Tori had written it to call him from Mrs. Bayfield's house.
   D. Tori had written it down to have Mrs. Bayfield scare him.

4. Why was Mrs. Bayfield sorry about having asked David to
   bring back the cane?
   A. She didn't really need the cane for walking.
   B. She had already bought a new cane.
   C. She had forgotten all about the cane.
   D. She hadn't wanted to see David hurt.

5. Why did Mrs. Bayfield say that David punished himself?
   A. He had a bad personality.
   B. He was a caring person.
   C. He wasn't very sensitive.
   D. He had a real curse on him.

6. What did David do with his project from shop class?
   A. He gave it to Tori as a heart.
   B. He gave it to Tori as a cheese board
   C. He added the stem back on it.
   D. He threw it away.

7. Which of the following is NOT one reason that we know
   David Ballinger became an important person in the future?
   A. His birthday was a holiday.
   B. He made a famous speech.
   C. Students looked up to him.
   D. He invented the word "drooble."

1분에 몇 단어를 읽는지 리딩 속도를 측정해보세요.

$$\frac{1{,}711 \text{ words}}{\text{reading time (\quad) sec}} \times 60 = (\qquad) \text{ WPM}$$

Build Your Vocabulary

chin ^{복습}
[tʃin]

n. 턱
Your chin is the part of your face that is below your mouth and above your neck.

ordinary ^{복습}
[ɔ́:rdənèri]

a. 보통의, 평범한
Ordinary people or things are normal and not special or different in any way.

rim ^{복습}
[rim]

n. (둥근 물건의) 가장자리, 테두리; **v.** 둘러싸다, 테를 두르다
The rim of a circular object is its outside edge.

draw ^{복습}
[drɔ:]

v. (drew–drawn) (사람의 마음을) 끌다; (연필·펜·분필 등으로) 그리다; **n.** 추첨, 제비 뽑기
If someone or something draws you, it attracts you very strongly.

rub ^{복습}
[rʌb]

v. 비비다, 문지르다; 스치다; **n.** 문지르기
If you rub a part of your body, you move your hand or fingers backwards and forwards over it while pressing firmly.

curse ^{복습}
[kə:rs]

n. 저주; 욕(설), 악담; **v.** 욕(설)을 하다; 저주를 내리다
If you say that there is a curse on someone, you mean that there seems to be a supernatural power causing unpleasant things to happen to them.

anxious ^{복습}
[ǽŋkʃəs]

a. 걱정하는, 염려하는; 열망하는, 간절히 바라는 (anxiously **ad.** 걱정스럽게)
If you are anxious to do something or anxious that something should happen, you very much want to do it or very much want it to happen.

squeeze ^{복습}
[skwi:z]

v. 꽉 쥐다, 짜다, 압착하다; 쑤셔 넣다; **n.** 압착, 짜냄
If you squeeze something, you press it firmly, usually with your hands.

couch ^{복습}
[kautʃ]

n. 소파, 긴 의자
A couch is a long, comfortable seat for two or three people.

bunch ^{복습}
[bʌntʃ]

v. 단단해지다, 단단하게 만들다; **n.** 다발, 묶음; (양·수가) 많음
(bunch together **idiom** 무리를 짓다, 함께 모이다)
If people bunch together, they move close together to form a tight group.

whisper ^{복습}
[hwíspər]

v. 속삭이다
When you whisper, you say something very quietly.

mutter ^{복습}
[mʌ́tər]

v. 중얼거리다; 투덜거리다; **n.** 중얼거림
If you mutter, you speak very quietly so that you cannot easily be heard, often because you are complaining about something.

cane ^{복습}
[kein]

n. 지팡이
A cane is a long thin stick with a curved or round top which you can use to support yourself when you are walking.

command ^{복습}
[kəmǽnd]

v. 명령하다, 지휘하다, 지배하다; **n.** 명령, 지휘
If someone in authority commands you to do something, they tell you that you must do it.

grab ^{복습}
[græb]

v. 붙잡다, 움켜잡다; **n.** 움켜잡으려고 함
If you grab something, you take it or pick it up suddenly and roughly.

leap ^{**}
[li:p]

v. 껑충 뛰다, 뛰어넘다; **n.** 뜀, 도약
If you leap, you jump high in the air or jump a long distance.

stare ^{복습}
[stɛər]

n. 빤히 쳐다보기, 응시; **v.** 빤히 쳐다보다, 응시하다
A stare is a long look at something or someone with your eyes wide open.

gasp ^{복습}
[gæsp]

v. 숨이 턱 막히다, 헉 하고 숨을 쉬다; **n.** (숨이 막히는 듯) 헉 하는 소리를 냄
When you gasp, you take a short quick breath through your mouth, especially when you are surprised, shocked, or in pain.

deliberate [*]
[dilíbərət]

a. 신중한, 계획적인 (deliberately **ad.** 신중하게, 계획적으로)
If you do something that is deliberate, you planned to do it beforehand, and so it happens on purpose.

rigid [*]
[rídʒid]

a. 굳은, 단단한; 엄격한, 완고한 (rigidly **ad.** 단단하고, 견고하게)
A rigid substance or object is stiff and does not bend, stretch, or twist easily.

freckle ^{복습}
[frekl]

n. 주근깨
Freckles are small light brown spots on someone's skin, especially on their face.

statue [*]
[stǽtʃu:]

n. 상(像), 조각상
A statue is a large sculpture of a person or an animal, made of stone or metal.

mess ^{복습}
[mes]

n. (지저분하고) 엉망(진창)인 상태; **v.** 엉망으로 만들다
If you say that a situation is a mess, you mean that it is full of trouble or problems.

in the first place ^{복습}

idiom 우선, 먼저
You say in the first place when you are talking about the beginning of a situation or about the situation as it was before a series of events.

sour ^{복습}
[sauər]

a. (맛이) 신, 시큼한
Something that is sour has a sharp, unpleasant taste like the taste of a lemon.

horrible ^{복습}
[hɔ́:rəbl]

a. 끔찍한, 소름 끼치게 싫은; 무서운
You can call something horrible when it causes you to feel great shock, fear, and disgust.

painful ^{**}
[péinfəl]

a. 아픈, 고통스러운
If a part of your body is painful, it hurts because it is injured or because there is something wrong with it.

heartbeat
[háːrtbìːt]

n. 심장 박동
Your heartbeat is the regular movement of your heart as it pumps blood around your body.

tremble[*]
[trembl]

v. 떨다, 떨리다 (trembling **a.** 떠는, 떨리는)
If you tremble, you shake slightly because you are frightened or cold.

attach[*]
[ətǽʧ]

v. 붙이다, 부착하다 (attached **a.** 붙여진)
If you attach something to an object, you connect it or fasten it to the object.

stiff[복습]
[stif]

a. 단단한, 뻣뻣한; 완강한, 완고한
Something that is stiff is firm or does not bend easily.

swoon
[swuːn]

v. 황홀해지다; 기절하다; **n.** 기절, 졸도; 황홀
If you swoon, you are strongly affected by your feelings for someone you love or admire very much.

faint[*]
[feint]

a. 희미한, 어렴풋한; **v.** 기절하다
A faint sound, color, mark, feeling, or quality has very little strength or intensity.

blink[*]
[bliŋk]

v. 눈을 깜박거리다; (등불·별 등이) 깜박이다; **n.** 깜박거림
When you blink or when you blink your eyes, you shut your eyes and very quickly open them again.

pretend[복습]
[priténd]

v. ~인 체하다, 가장하다; **a.** 가짜의, 꾸민
If you pretend that something is the case, you act in a way that is intended to make people believe that it is the case, although in fact it is not.

assure[복습]
[əʃúər]

v. 안심시키다; 보증하다
If you assure someone that something is true or will happen, you tell them that it is definitely true or will definitely happen, often in order to make them less worried.

witch[복습]
[witʃ]

n. 마녀
In fairy stories, a witch is a woman, usually an old woman, who has evil magic powers.

give away

idiom (비밀을) 누설하다, 드러내다
If something gives away, it does or says something that shows its secret.

glance[복습]
[glæns]

v. 흘긋 보다, 잠깐 보다; **n.** 흘긋 봄
If you glance at something or someone, you look at them very quickly and then look away again immediately.

petrify
[pétrəfài]

v. 겁에 질리게 만들다; 석화하다 (petrified **a.** 극도로 무서워하는)
If something petrifies you, it makes you feel very frightened.

blush[복습]
[blʌʃ]

v. 얼굴을 붉히다, 얼굴이 빨개지다; **n.** (당황하거나 수치스러워) 얼굴이 붉어짐
When you blush, your face becomes redder than usual because you are ashamed or embarrassed.

shrug[복습]
[ʃrʌg]

v. (양 손바닥을 내보이면서 어깨를) 으쓱하다; **n.** (어깨를) 으쓱하기
If you shrug, you raise your shoulders to show that you are not interested in something or that you do not know or care about something.

compatriot
[kəmpéitriət]

n. 동포
Your compatriots are people from your own country.

regurgitate ^{복습}
[rigə:rdʒətèit]

v. (삼킨 음식물을 입 안으로 다시) 역류시키다;
(듣거나 읽은 내용을 별 생각 없이) 반복하다
If a person or animal regurgitates food, they bring it back up from their stomach before it has been digested.

rant
[rænt]

v. 고함치다, 큰소리로 불평하다
To speak or shout in a loud, uncontrolled or angry way, often saying confused or foolish things.

rave
[reiv]

v. 횡설수설하다, 헛소리를 하다; 열변을 토하다
If someone raves, they talk in an excited and uncontrolled way.

utter*
[ʌ́tər]

① a. 완전한, 전적인, 절대적인 ② v. 발언하다, 입을 열다
You use utter to emphasize that something is great in extent, degree, or amount.

astonish*
[əstániʃ]

v. 깜짝 놀라게 하다 (astonishment n. 놀람)
If something or someone astonishes you, they surprise you very much.

exclaim ^{복습}
[ikskléim]

v. 외치다, 소리치다
If you exclaim, you say or shout something suddenly because of surprise, fear and pleasure.

coincidence ^{복습}
[kouínsidəns]

n. (우연의) 일치, 부합; 동시에 일어남
A coincidence is when two or more similar or related events occur at the same time by chance and without any planning.

weird ^{복습}
[wiərd]

a. 이상한, 기묘한; 수상한
If you describe something or someone as weird, you mean that they are strange.

bruise ^{복습}
[bru:z]

v. 멍들게 하다, 타박상을 입히다; n. 타박상, 멍 (bruised a. 멍든)
If you bruise a part of your body, a bruise appears on it, for example because something hits you. If you bruise easily, bruises appear when something hits you only slightly.

shiver*
[ʃívər]

v. (추위·공포로) 후들후들 떨다; 전율하다; n. 떨림, 전율
When you shiver, your body shakes slightly because you are cold or frightened.

stand up to ^{복습}

idiom (용감히) 맞서다
If you stand up to someone or something, you resist them or defend your position against them.

1분에 몇 단어를 읽는지 리딩 속도를 측정해보세요.

$$\frac{703 \text{ words}}{\text{reading time ( ) sec}} \times 60 = (\quad) \text{ WPM}$$

Build Your Vocabulary

ordinary ^{복습}
[ɔ́:rdənèri]

a. 보통의, 평범한
Ordinary people or things are normal and not special or different in any way.

rim ^{복습}
[rim]

n. (둥근 물건의) 가장자리, 테두리; **v.** 둘러싸다, 테를 두르다
The rim of a circular object is its outside edge.

brag ^{복습}
[bræg]

v. 자랑하다, 자만하다, 허풍떨다
If you brag, you say in a very proud way that you have something or have done something.

offer ^{복습}
[ɔ́:fər]

v. 제안하다; 제공하다; **n.** 제공
If you offer something to someone, you ask them if they would like to have it or use it.

part ***
[pa:rt]

v. (~와) 헤어지다; **n.** 일부, 약간; 부분
When two people part, or if one person parts from another, they leave each other.

compare ^{복습}
[kəmpέər]

v. 비교하다, 대조하다; 비유하다
When you compare things, you consider them and discover the differences or similarities between them

shrug ^{복습}
[ʃrʌg]

v. (양 손바닥을 내보이면서 어깨를) 으쓱하다; **n.** (어깨를) 으쓱하기
If you shrug, you raise your shoulders to show that you are not interested in something or that you do not know or care about something.

freckle ^{복습}
[frekl]

n. 주근깨
Freckles are small light brown spots on someone's skin, especially on their face.

count ^{복습}
[kaunt]

v. 수를 세다, 계산하다; 중요하다; (정식으로) 인정되다; **n.** 셈, 계산
When you count, you say all the numbers one after another up to a particular number.

pitcher ^{복습}
[pítʃər]

① **n.** 물 주전자 ② **n.** 투수, 피처
A pitcher is a jug.

poet ^{복습}
[póuit]

n. 시인
A poet is a person who writes poems.

ignore ^{복습}
[ignɔ́:r]

v. 무시하다
If you ignore someone or something, you pay no attention to them.

weird^{복습}
[wiərd]

a. 이상한, 기묘한; 수상한
If you describe something or someone as weird, you mean that they are strange.

coincidence^{복습}
[kouínsidəns]

n. (우연의) 일치, 부합; 동시에 일어남
A coincidence is when two or more similar or related events occur at the same time by chance and without any planning.

flour^{복습}
[fláuər]

n. 밀가루; 분말, 가루
Flour is a white or brown powder that is made by grinding grain, which is used to make bread, cakes, and pastry.

sensitive^{복습}
[sénsitiv]

a. 민감한, 예민한; 감수성이 강한
If you are sensitive to other people's needs, problems, or feelings, you show understanding and awareness of them.

guilt^{복습}
[gilt]

n. 유죄, 죄책감 (guity **a.** 유죄의, 죄책감이 드는)
Guilt is the fact that you have done something wrong or illegal.

punish^{복습}
[pʌ́niʃ]

v. 벌하다, 응징하다, 처벌하다 (punishment **n.** 벌, 처벌)
To punish someone means to make them suffer in some way because they have done something wrong.

subconscious
[sʌbkánʃəs]

n. 잠재의식; **a.** 잠재의식적인
Your subconscious is the part of your mind that can influence you or affect your behavior even though you are not aware of it.

obvious^{복습}
[ábviəs]

a. 명백한, 분명한 (obviously **ad.** 분명히, 명백하게)
If something is obvious, it is easy to see or understand.

thoughtful[*]
[θɔ́:tfəl]

a. 사려 깊은; (조용히) 생각에 잠긴
If you describe someone as thoughtful, you approve of them because they remember what other people want, need, or feel, and try not to upset them.

considerate[*]
[kənsídərət]

a. 사려 깊은, (남을) 배려하는
Someone who is considerate pays attention to the needs, wishes, or feelings of other people.

beam^{복습}
[bi:m]

v. 활짝 웃다; **n.** 빛줄기
If you say that someone is beaming, you mean that they have a big smile on their face because they are happy, pleased, or proud about something.

1분에 몇 단어를 읽는지 리딩 속도를 측정해보세요.

$$\frac{465 \text{ words}}{\text{reading time ( ) sec}} \times 60 = (\quad) \text{ WPM}$$

Build Your Vocabulary

curse ^{복습}
[kə:rs]

n. 저주; 욕(설), 악담; **v.** 욕(설)을 하다; 저주를 내리다
If you say that there is a curse on someone, you mean that there seems to be a supernatural power causing unpleasant things to happen to them.

on the other hand ^{복습}

idiom 다른 한편으로는, 반면에
You use on the other hand to introduce the second of two contrasting points, facts, or ways of looking at something.

stuff ^{복습}
[stʌf]

n. 물건, 물질; **v.** 채워 넣다, 속을 채우다
You can use stuff to refer to things such as a substance, a collection of things, events, or ideas in a general way without mentioning the thing itself by name.

subconscious ^{복습}
[sʌbkánʃəs]

n. 잠재의식; **a.** 잠재의식적인
Your subconscious is the part of your mind that can influence you or affect your behavior even though you are not aware of it.

flip off ^{복습}

idiom 손가락으로 욕을 하다
If you flip someone off, you raise your middle finger to them in a very rude sign.

punish ^{복습}
[pʌniʃ]

v. 벌하다, 응징하다, 처벌하다
To punish someone means to make them suffer in some way because they have done something wrong.

strike ^{복습}
[straik]

v. (struck–stricken/struck) 발생하다, 덮치다; 갑자기 떠오르다; 치다, 부딪치다; **n.** 파업; 공격, 공습
If something such as an illness or disaster strikes, it suddenly happens.

one way or another

idiom 어떻게든, 그럭저럭
You can use one way or another when you want to say that something definitely happens, but without giving any details about how it happens.

recess ^{복습}
[risés]

n. (학교의) 쉬는 시간; 휴회
A recess is a short period of time when you have a rest or a change from what you are doing, especially if you are working or if you are in a boring or unpleasant situation.

tense ^{복습}
[tens]

v. 긴장하다; 긴장시키다, 팽팽하게 하다; **a.** 긴장한, 긴박한; 팽팽한
If your muscles tense, if you tense, or if you tense your muscles, your muscles become tight and stiff, often because you are anxious or frightened.

bother ^{복습}
[báðər]

v. 신경 쓰다, 애를 쓰다; 귀찮게 하다, 귀찮게 말을 걸다; **n.** 성가심
If you do not bother to do something or if you do not bother with it, you do not do it, consider it, or use it because you think it is unnecessary or because you are too lazy.

athlete *
[ǽθliːt]

n. 운동선수, 스포츠맨
A person who is very good at sports, especially one who competes in organized events.

hardly ^{복습}
[háːrdli]

ad. 거의 ~아니다, 전혀 ~않다
When you say you can hardly do something, you are emphasizing that it is very difficult for you to do it.

poet ^{복습}
[póuit]

n. 시인
A poet is a person who writes poems.

fly ^{복습}
[flai]

n. (바지 앞의) 지퍼로 잠그는 부분; 파리; **v.** (새 · 곤충이) 날다
The front opening on a pair of trousers is referred to as the fly. It usually consists of a zip or row of buttons behind a band of cloth.

offend ^{복습}
[əfénd]

v. 기분을 상하게 하다, 불쾌하게 하다
If you offend someone, you say or do something rude which upsets or embarrasses them.

1분에 몇 단어를 읽는지 리딩 속도를 측정해보세요.

$$\frac{417 \text{ words}}{\text{reading time (\quad) sec}} \times 60 = (\quad) \text{ WPM}$$

Build Your Vocabulary

ignore 복습
[ignóːr]

v. 무시하다
If you ignore someone or something, you pay no attention to them.

redden 복습
[rédn]

v. 빨개지다, 붉어지다
If someone reddens or their face reddens, their face turns pink or red, often because they are embarrassed or angry.

quack
[kwæk]

v. (오리가) 꽥꽥거리다; **n.** (오리가) 꽥꽥 우는 소리
When a duck quacks, it makes the noise that ducks typically make.

trip 복습
[tríp]

n. 여행; **v.** 걸려 넘어지다; 경쾌한 걸음걸이로 걷다 (field trip **n.** 현장 학습)
A trip is a journey that you make to a particular place.

flip someone off 복습

idiom 손가락으로 욕을 하다
If you flip someone off, you raise your middle finger to them in a very rude sign.

attention 복습
[əténʃən]

n. 주의 (집중), 주목
If you give someone or something your attention, you look at it, listen to it, or think about it carefully.

stare 복습
[stɛər]

v. 빤히 쳐다보다, 응시하다; **n.** 빤히 쳐다보기, 응시
If you stare at someone or something, you look at them for a long time.

bet 복습
[bet]

v. (~이) 틀림없다; (경마 · 내기 등에) 돈을 걸다; **n.** 내기; 내기 돈
You use expressions such as 'I bet,' 'I'll bet,' and 'you can bet' to indicate that you are sure something is true.

memorize 복습
[méməràiz]

v. 암기하다
If you memorize something, you learn it so that you can remember it exactly.

recite 복습
[risáit]

v. 암송하다, 낭독하다; 죽 말하다
When someone recites a poem or other piece of writing, they say it aloud after they have learned it.

dignity 복습
[dígnəti]

n. 위엄, 품위; 존엄성
If someone behaves or moves with dignity, they are calm, controlled, and admirable.

grace 복습
[greis]

n. 품위; 우아함
If someone behaves with grace, they behave in a pleasant, polite, and dignified way, even when they are upset or being treated unfairly.

pound ^{복습}
[paund]

① v. 쿵쿵 울리다, 마구 치다, 세게 두드리다; n. 타격 ② n. 파운드(무게의 단위)
③ n. 주인 잃은 개 보호소
If you pound something or pound on it, you hit it with great force, usually loudly and repeatedly.

grip ^{복습}
[grip]

v. 꽉 잡다, 움켜잡다; n. 잡음, 움켜쥠; 손잡이
If you grip something, you take hold of it with your hand and continue to hold it firmly.

exhibit**
[igzíbit]

n. 전시, 전람; v. 전시하다, 나타내다
An exhibit is a painting, sculpture, or object of interest that is displayed to the public in a museum or art gallery.

blush ^{복습}
[blʌʃ]

v. 얼굴을 붉히다, 얼굴이 빨개지다; n. (당황하거나 수치스러워) 얼굴이 붉어짐
When you blush, your face becomes redder than usual because you are ashamed or embarrassed.

bounce ^{복습}
[bauns]

v. 튀다, 튀게 하다; 급히 움직이다, 뛰어다니다; n. 튐, 바운드
If something bounces off a surface or is bounced off it, it reaches the surface and is reflected back.

whisper ^{복습}
[hwíspər]

v. 속삭이다
When you whisper, you say something very quietly.

수고하셨습니다!

드디어 끝까지 다 읽으셨군요! 축하드립니다! 여러분은 이 책을 통해 총 39,823개의 단어를 읽으셨고, 800개 이상의 어휘와 표현들을 익히셨습니다. 이 책에 나온 어휘는 다른 원서를 읽을 때에도 빈번히 만날 수 있는 필수 어휘들입니다. 이 책을 읽었던 경험은 비슷한 수준의 다른 원서들을 읽을 때 큰 도움이 될 것입니다. 이제 자신의 상황에 맞게 원서를 반복해서 읽거나, 오디오북을 들어 볼 수 있습니다. 혹은 비슷한 수준의 다른 원서를 찾아 읽는 것도 좋습니다. 일단 원서를 완독한 뒤에 어떻게 계속 영어 공부를 이어갈 수 있을지, 아래에 제시되는 도움말을 꼼꼼히 살펴보고 각자 상황에 맞게 적용해 보세요!

리딩(Reading)을 확실하게 다지고 싶다면? 반복해서 읽어 보세요!

리딩 실력을 탄탄하게 다지고 싶다면, 같은 원서를 2~3번 반복해서 읽을 것을 권합니다. 같은 책을 여러 번 읽으면 지루할 것 같지만, 꼭 그렇지도 않습니다. 반복해서 읽을 때 처음과 주안점을 다르게 두면, 전혀 다른 느낌으로 재미있게 읽을 수 있습니다.

처음 원서를 읽을 때는 생소한 단어들과 스토리로 인해 읽으면서 곧바로 이해하기가 매우 힘들 수 있습니다. 전체 맥락을 잡고 읽어도 약간 버거운 느낌이지요. 하지만 반복해서 읽기 시작하면 달라집니다. 일단 내용을 파악한 상황이기 때문에 문장 구조나 어휘의 활용에 더 집중하게 되고, 조금 더 깊이 있게 읽을 수 있습니다. 좋은 표현과 문장을 수집하고 메모할 만한 여유도 생기게 되지요. 어휘도 많이 익숙해졌기 때문에 리딩 속도에도 탄력이 붙습니다. 처음 읽을 때는 '내용'에서 재미를 느꼈다면, 반복해서 읽을 때에는 '영어'에서 재미를 느끼게 되는 것입니다. 따라서 리딩 실력을 더욱 확고하게 다지고자 한다면, 같은 책을 2~3회 정도 반복해서 읽을 것을 권해 드립니다.

많은 영어 학습자들이 '리스닝이 안 돼서 문제'라고 한탄합니다. 그리고 리스닝 실력을 늘리는 방법으로 무슨 뜻인지 몰라도 반복해서 듣는 '무작정 듣기'를 선택합니다. 하지만 뜻도 모르면서 무작정 듣는 일에는 엄청난 인내력이 필요합니다. 그래서 대부분 며칠 시도하다가 포기해 버리고 말지요.

따라서 모르는 내용을 무작정 듣는 것보다는 어느 정도 알고 있는 내용을 반복해서 듣는 것이 더 효과적인 듣기 방법입니다. 그리고 이런 방식의 듣기에 활용할 수 있는 가장 좋은 교재가 오디오북입니다.

리스닝 실력을 향상하고 싶다면, 이 책에서 제공하는 오디오북을 이용해서 듣는 연습을 해 보세요. 활용법은 간단합니다. 일단 책을 한 번 완독했다면, 오디오북을 통해 다시 들어 보는 것입니다. 휴대 기기에 넣어 시간이 날 때 틈틈이 듣는 것도 좋고, 책상에 앉아 눈으로는 텍스트를 보며 귀로 읽는 것도 좋습니다. 이미 읽었던 내용이라 이해하기가 훨씬 수월하고, 애매했던 발음들도 자연스럽게 교정할 수 있습니다. 또 성우의 목소리 연기를 듣다 보면 내용이 더욱 생동감 있게 다가와 이해도가 높아지는 효과도 거둘 수 있습니다.

반대로 듣기에 자신 있는 사람이라면, 책을 읽기 전에 처음부터 오디오북을 먼저 듣는 것도 좋은 방법입니다. 귀를 통해 책을 쭉 읽어 보고, 이후에 다시 눈으로 책을 읽으면서 잘 들리지 않았던 부분을 보충하는 것이지요.

중요한 것은 내용을 따라가면서, 내용에 푹 빠져서 반복해 들어야 한다는 것입니다. 이렇게 연습을 반복해서 눈으로 읽지 않은 책이라도 '귀를 통해' 읽을 수 있을 정도가 되면, 리스닝으로 고생하는 일은 거의 없을 것입니다.

왼쪽의 QR 코드를 스마트폰으로 인식하여
정식 오디오북을 들어 보세요!
더불어 롱테일북스 홈페이지(www.longtailbooks.co.kr)에서도
오디오북 MP3 파일을 다운로드 받을 수 있습니다.

스피킹(Speaking)이 고민이라면? 소리 내어 읽어 보세요!

스피킹 역시 많은 학습자들이 고민하는 부분입니다. 스피킹이 고민이라면, 원서를 큰 소리로 읽는 낭독 훈련(voice reading)을 해 보세요!

'소리 내어 읽는 것이 말하기에 정말로 도움이 될까?'라고 의아한 생각이 들 수도 있습니다. 하지만 인간의 두뇌 입장에서 봤을 때, 성대 구조를 활용해서 '발화'한다는 점에서는 소리 내어 읽기와 말하기에 큰 차이가 없다고 합니다. 소리 내어 읽는 것은 '타인의 생각'을 전달하고, 직접 말하는 것은 '자신의 생각'을 전달한다는 차이가 있을 뿐, 머릿속에서 문장을 처리하고 조음기관(혀와 성대 등)을 움직여 의미를 만든다는 점에서 같은 과정인 것이지요. 따라서 소리 내어 읽는 연습을 꾸준히 하는 것은 스피킹 연습에 큰 도움이 됩니다.

소리 내어 읽기를 하는 방법은 간단합니다. 일단 오디오북을 들으면서 성우의 목소리를 최대한 따라 하며 같이 읽어 보세요. 발음뿐 아니라 억양, 어조, 느낌까지 완벽히 따라 한다고 생각하면서 소리 내어 읽습니다. 따라 읽는 것이 조금 익숙해지면, 옆의 누군가에게 이 책을 읽어 준다는 생각으로 소리 내어 계속 읽어 나갑니다. 한 번 눈과 귀로 읽었던 책이기 때문에 보다 수월하게 진행할 수 있고, 자연스럽게 어휘와 표현을 복습하는 효과도 거두게 됩니다. 또 이렇게 소리 내어 읽은 것을 녹음해서 들어 보면 스스로에게도 좋은 피드백이 됩니다.

최근 말하기가 강조되면서 소리 내어 읽기가 크게 각광을 받고 있긴 하지만, 그렇다고 소리 내어 읽기가 무조건 좋은 것만은 아닙니다. 책을 소리 내어 읽다 보면, 무의식적으로 속으로 발음을 하는 습관을 가지게 되어 리딩 속도 자체는 오히려 크게 떨어지는 현상이 발생할 수 있습니다. 따라서 빠른 리딩 속도가 중요한 수험생이나 고학력 학습자들에게는 소리 내어 읽기가 적절하지 않은 방법입니다. 효과가 좋다는 말만 믿고 무턱대고 따라 하기보다는 자신의 필요에 맞게 우선순위를 정하고 원서를 활용하는 것이 좋습니다.

라이팅(Writing)까지 욕심이 난다면? 요약하는 연습을 해 보세요!

원서를 라이팅 연습에 직접적으로 활용하는 데에는 한계가 있지만, 적절히 활용하면 원서도 유용한 라이팅 자료가 될 수 있습니다.

특히 책을 읽고 그 내용을 요약하는 연습은 큰 도움이 됩니다. 요약 훈련의 방식도 간단합니다. 원서를 읽고 그날 읽은 분량만큼 혹은 책을 다 읽고 전체 내용을 기반으로, 책 내용을 한번 요약하고 나의 느낌을 영어로 적어 보는 것입니다.

이때 그 책에 나왔던 단어와 표현을 최대한 활용하여 요약하는 것이 중요합니다. 영어 표현력은 결국 얼마나 다양한 어휘로 많은 표현을 해 보았느냐가 좌우하게 됩니다. 이런 면에서 내가 읽은 책을, 그 책에 나온 문장과 어휘로 다시 표현해 보는 것은 매우 효율적인 방법입니다. 책에 나온 어휘와 표현을 단순히 읽고 무슨 말인지 아는 정도가 아니라, 실제로 직접 활용해서 쓸 수 있을 만큼 확실하게 익히게 되는 것이지요. 여기에 첨삭까지 받을 수 있는 방법이 있다면 금상첨화입니다.

이러한 '표현하기' 연습은 스피킹 훈련에도 그대로 적용될 수 있습니다. 책을 읽고 그 내용을 3분 안에 다른 사람에게 영어로 말하는 연습을 해 보세요. 순발력과 표현력을 기르는 좋은 훈련이 될 것입니다.

꾸준히 원서를 읽고 싶다면? 뉴베리 수상작을 계속 읽어 보세요!

뉴베리 상이 세계 최고 권위의 아동 문학상인 만큼, 그 수상작들은 확실히 완성도를 검증받은 작품이라고 할 수 있습니다. 특히 '쉬운 어휘로 쓰인 깊이 있는 문장'으로 이루어졌다는 점이 영어 학습자들에게 큰 호응을 얻고 있습니다. 이렇게 '검증된 원서'를 꾸준히 읽는 것은 영어 실력 향상에 큰 도움이 됩니다.

아래에 수준별로 제시된 뉴베리 수상작 목록을 보며 적절한 책들을 찾아 계속 읽어 보세요. 꼭 뉴베리 수상작이 아니더라도 마음에 드는 작가의 다른 책을 읽어 보는 것 또한 아주 좋은 방법입니다.

• 영어 초보자도 쉽게 읽을 만한 아주 쉬운 수준. 소리 내어 읽기에도 아주 적합.

Sarah, Plain and Tall ★(Medal, 8,331단어), The Hundred Penny Box (Honor, 5,878단어), The Hundred Dresses ★(Honor, 7,329단어), My Father's Dragon (Honor, 7,682단어), 26 Fairmount Avenue (Honor, 6,737단어)

- 중 · 고등학생 정도 영어 학습자라면 쉽게 읽을 수 있는 수준. 소리 내어 읽기에도 비교적 적합한 편.

Because of Winn-Dixie★ (Honor, 22,123단어), What Jamie Saw (Honor, 17,203단어), Charlotte's Web (Honor, 31,938단어), Dear Mr. Henshaw (Medal, 18,145단어), Missing May (Medal, 17,509단어)

- 대학생 정도 영어 학습자라면 무난한 수준. 소리 내어 읽기에는 적합하지 않음.

Number The Stars★ (Medal, 27,197단어), A Single Shard (Medal, 33,726단어), The Tale of Despereaux★ (Medal, 32,375단어), Hatchet★ (Medal, 42,328단어), Bridge to Terabithia (Medal, 32,888단어), A Fine White Dust (Honor, 19,022단어), Jennifer, Hecate, Macbeth, William McKinley and Me, Elizabeth (Honor, 23,266단어)

- 원서 완독 경험을 가진 학습자에게 적절한 수준. 소리 내어 읽기에는 적합하지 않음.

The Giver★ (Medal, 43,617단어), From the Mixed-Up Files of Mrs. Basil E. Frankweiler (Medal, 30,906단어), The View from Saturday (Medal, 42,685단어), Holes★ (Medal, 47,079단어), Criss Cross (Medal, 48,221단어), Walk Two Moons (Medal, 59,400단어), The Graveyard Book (Medal, 67,380단어)

뉴베리 수상작과 뉴베리 수상 작가의 좋은 작품을 엄선한 「뉴베리 컬렉션」에도 위 목록에 있는 도서 중 상당수가 포함될 예정입니다.

★ 「뉴베리 컬렉션」으로 이미 출간된 도서

어떤 책들이 출간되었는지 확인하려면, 지금 인터넷 서점에서
뉴베리 컬렉션을 검색해 보세요.

뉴베리 수상작을 동영상 강의로 만나 보세요!

영어원서 전문 동영상 강의 사이트 영서당(yseodang.com)에서는 뉴베리 컬렉션 『Holes』, 『Because of Winn-Dixie』, 『The Miraculous Journey of Edward Tulane』, 『Wayside School 시리즈』 등의 동영상 강의를 제공하고 있습니다. 뉴베리 수상작이라는 최고의 영어 교재와 EBS 출신 인기 강사가 만난 명강의! 지금 사이트를 방문해서 무료 샘플 강의를 들어 보세요!

'스피드 리딩 카페'를 통해 원서 읽기 습관을 길러 보세요!

일상에서 영어를 한마디도 쓰지 않는 비영어권 국가에서 살고 있는 우리가 영어 환경에 가장 쉽고, 편하고, 부담 없이 노출되는 방법은 바로 '영어원서 읽기'입니다. 언제 어디서든 원서를 붙잡고 읽기만 하면 곧바로 영어를 접하는 환경이 만들어지기 때문이지요. 하루에 20분씩만 꾸준히 읽는다면, 1년에 무려 120시간 동안 영어에 노출될 수 있습니다. 이러한 이유 때문에 영어 교육 전문가들이 영어 원서 읽기를 추천하는 것이지요.

하지만 원서 읽기가 좋다는 것을 알아도 막상 꾸준히 읽는 것은 쉽지 않습니다. 그럴 때에는 13만 명 이상의 회원을 보유한 국내 최대 원서 읽기 동호회 <스피드 리딩 카페> (cafe.naver. com/readingtc)를 방문해 보세요.

원서별로 정리된 무료 PDF 단어장과 수준별 추천 원서 목록 등 유용한 자료는 물론, 뉴베리 수상작을 포함한 다양한 원서의 리뷰를 무료로 확인할 수 있습니다. 특히 함께 모여서 원서를 읽는 '북클럽'은 중간에 포기하지 않고 원서를 끝까지 읽는 습관을 기르는 데 큰 도움이 될 것입니다.

chapters 1 to 4

1. C   They had come to steal her cane.

2. D   David laughed too, even though he didn't think it was funny. Mrs. Bayfield wasn't ugly. She was just a lonely old lady who dressed kind of weird.

3. A   But he knew the reason he had given Mrs. Bayfield the finger was to try to impress Roger. What do I care what Roger thinks? he asked himself. Except he did care, and he knew it.

4. B   They threw the baseball back and forth in the backyard. In a way David felt like he was doing a good deed to make up for the bad deed he had done earlier. He knew how much Ricky looked up to him.

5. C   It didn't seem right. I should have gotten in trouble, David thought. It was my fault. I broke the window. And Elizabeth could have gotten hurt. What if the ball hit her on the head or a piece of glass got in her eye? Besides, what kind of lesson was that for Ricky? He has to learn responsibility. If you do something wrong, even if it's not on purpose, you still have to suffer the consequences. I should have been punished, he thought.

6. B   Since the second grade David had stopped by Scott's house every morning on the way to school.

7. D   He toppled over in his chair. Miss Williams stopped reciting. Several kids were laughing. "Stay where you are, Mr. Ballinger," ordered Mr. MacFarland. "Huh?" "Maybe this will teach you to sit like a human being. Please continue, Miss Williams."

chapters 5 to 8

1. A   At the beginning of the year everyone had to sign up for either home economics1 or shop. There was no rule that boys had to take shop and girls had to take home ec. In fact, David shared his worktable with a girl. But girls can get away with doing "boy" things a lot easier than boys can get away with doing "girl" things. Shop was

David's worst subject. He would have liked to have taken home ec. He knew he'd have to know how to cook some day. But he could just imagine what the other kids would have called him if he had signed up for home ec.

2. B   "Is that for your girlfriend?asked Mo. "Huh?" said David. "I don't know." He shrugged. "Maybe." He was flattered that Mo would think he was the kind of guy who had a girlfriend. "Are you going to carve your initials in it?" she asked. "Why would I do that?" he asked. "She knows who I am." Whoever she was. "Isn't that what you're supposed to do with hearts?" asked Mo. She returned to her project. Wham! Wham! Wham! He watched her bang another nail in the back of the doghouse, then glanced back down at his own measly project. It did look more like a heart than an apple.

3. C   "Sorry I didn't wait for you this morning,said Scott. "It's not that I don't like you. I mean you're still my friend, it's just that, you know, it's not good for my reputation. I have to think of myself, too. You understand, right?

4. A   Maybe I really am cursed, he thought, picking at his dinner. I've got no friends. My mother hates me. In an odd way it made him feel better to pretend to believe Mrs. Bayfield put a curse on him. It gave him an excuse. It's not my fault I'm a dipshit. There's a curse on me.

5. B   David's mother was quite delighted to find out it was just an experiment. She was flattered that David didn't think she'd know what it meant.

6. C   David carried Scott's lunch all the way to school, where he saw Scott, Roger, Randy, and Alvin all laughing together. He dropped Scott's lunch into a trash can. After all, he didn't want to ruin Scott's reputation.

7. B   She did say hi to me, David realized. That was something. He wished he knew her first name. He wondered if he had ever heard it before. He went through every girl's name he could think of to see if one rang a bell. Alice Williams. Amy Williams. Betty Williams. Barbara Williams. Carol Williams. Cathy Williams. Debbie Williams. Donna Williams. He made it all the way through Zelda Williams, but the only bell that rang was the one at the end of the period.

chapters 9 to 12

1. B   Just one shot, hoped David as he wiped the sweat from his face. One clear shot to kick a goal past him. Or maybe just kick it right at him, as hard as he could, right into the middle of Roger Delbrook's smug face.

2. A   He stopped. Miss Williams was holding the soccer ball. She had freckles on her arms and legs, too. Up till now he hadn't even known she was in his P.E. class. He stared

at her with his mouth open and sweat dripping down his face. Besides her blue shorts and white button-down shirt, she wore a green headband and red high-top sneakers. She underhanded the soccer ball to him. He exhaled. "Thanks," he said. "You're welcome, Mr. Ballinger." Her green eyes sparkled as she smiled at him. He returned to the soccer game elated.

3. C   "Zeeper?" asked David, still not knowing what she was talking about. "I need to lift up my zeeper?" Suddenly he turned bright red. As inconspicuously as possible, he zipped his fly. "Gracias," said Mrs. Guiterrez. The class was hysterical.

4. B   "Yeah," David agreed as if he had also seen twenty-three naked girls before. "I can bring the pictures tomorrow," said Larry, "if you want to see 'em."

5. D   True, some of the same things that happened to Mrs. Bayfield happened to him, but that was just a coincidence. In a world where so many things are happening to so many people all the time, coincidences are bound to happen now and then.

6. C   He thought about everything that had happened to him: breaking the window, falling over in his chair, flipping off his mother, his fly.

7. A   All of his own problems suddenly seemed petty and insignificant to him, especially his so-called curse.

chapters 13 to 16

1. D   David shrugged. It was a lot easier for her to stand up to them than it was for him, he thought. They were not going to fight a girl.

2. B   David looked at the doghouse with the nameplate KILLER nailed above the entrance. "So what kind of dog do you have?he asked. "What?" asked Mo. "Oh, this." She glanced at her project. "I don't have a dog."

3. A   Science made sense. It was logical. It was consistent. If you dropped a rock, gravity would always cause it to fall down. It wouldn't sometimes fall up. If you combine two parts hydrogen with one part oxygen, you'll always get water. You won't sometimes get milk. Maybe that's why it was David's favorite subject. Nothing else in his life seemed to make sense anymore.

4. C   "You know, if someone else did it,said David a little later while eating lunch with Larry, "Everyone would have thought it was funny. Like if Roger Delbrook had done it, everybody would think it was real cool. He'd be bragging about it. 'You hear about how I made a stink bomb in Lugano's class?' But because I did it, then it's not cool. It's, Did you hear what that stinkpot Ballinger did now?"

5. C   "God, you're lucky!" said Larry. "Don't you think she's pretty? And she's really

funny, too." "Um, sure," said David. "I never really thought of her like that. I mean, being in shop, I guess because she's always hammering and stuff like that." Larry sighed. "Maybe if her hair wasn't so short—" David started to say. "I like her hair like that," said Larry. "That's how girls wear their hair in France."

6. D   Well, there is one thing for certain, he decided. I am not, not, not going to pour lemonade on my head.

7. A   He wanted to ask her why she built a doghouse if she didn't have a dog, but he was afraid she would take it the wrong way. "I'll help you carry it," he said. She looked at him in surprise. "You?" she asked. He didn't know if she was surprised that he would help her or because she thought he was a wimp and didn't think he could carry the heavy wooden doghouse. "I could probably get a friend of mine to help, too," he said slyly. "Larry Clarksdale. Do you know him?"

chapters 17 to 20

1. C   "Water?" "Okay." Mo reached behind a bush and turned on the hose. She took a drink from it, then handed it to David.

2. D   Mo turned off the hose. "I want to get a dog," she explained, "but so far my parents won't let me. But once they see this neat doghouse, they have to let me get a dog, right? I mean, what good's a doghouse without a dog?"

3. A   "I've seen you and Tori making moon eyes at each other," said Mo.

4. B   "You can put your books in my locker if you want," said Tori Williams.

5. A   David noticed that Ginger was wearing Scott's fringed leather jacket. That meant Scott was now going steady with one of the most popular girls in school.

6. D   "I was just wondering about something. We were talking about famous comedians today at school. Urn, who are The Three Stooges?"

7. A   David didn't like saying mean things about Mrs. Bayfield, but he had to convince his friends she was really a witch. Little did he know that one day his own face would be hanging on the wall of her house.

chapters 21 to 24

1. A   "How about you, Randy?" Scott asked. "Why don't you and Tori join us?" He said the name Tori especially loud. "Yeah, that Tori Williams is one hot babe!" said Roger.

2. C   "You shouldn't have stepped out of their way," said Larry. "Huh?" "You lost face," said Larry.

3. B   "I don't have to fight. I know kung fu." "Yeah, right," said David.

4. B   Friday afternoon and evening David couldn't stop thinking about Tori—and Randy. What if he really did ask her out? What would she say to him? She might be talking on the phone to him right now. Saturday he worried about their date. He wondered where they went, what movie they saw. Was it rated R? What else did they do? Did he put his arm around her? He might be kissing her right now. Sunday he wondered if she was in love with him. What if she came to school wearing Randy's jacket? She wouldn't be allowed to talk to him anymore, not even "Hello, Mr. Ballinger."

5. D   "You have to pour a pitcher of lemonade on your head," said Larry. He smiled, proud behind his blue sunglasses. "Are you crazy?" asked David. "Mrs. Bayfield put a boomerang curse on you," Larry explained. "They're actually pretty common in Australia." "Larry lived in Australia for six months," said Mo. Somehow, David wasn't surprised. "Everything you did to Mrs. Bayfield has happened to you, right?" Larry asked him. "It's the classic Australian boomerang curse. Except you haven't poured a pitcher of lemonade on your head. Once you do that, the boomerang will have gone full circle and the curse will be over."

6. C   "You're a stooge!" said Ricky. "Look, just because Roger calls me names. That's his problem. Names don't hurt me." "But it's true!" said Ricky. "You are a stooge. I saw you and your stoogy friends. You dumped a whole pitcher of pink lemonade on your head."

7. D   "I was just thinking," Larry said to Mo. "Maybe you and I could pretend to be on a date, too. We wouldn't really be on a date. We'd just pretend to be on a date." He adjusted his blue sunglasses. "Like, if David wants to put his arm around Tori, or something, he can signal me, and then I'll put my arm around you. I'll just be pretending, but Tori won't know that." "Oh, well, sure, if it will make it easier for David," said Mo. "Sure."

chapters 25 to 28

1. B   He never called her. There were more than two pages of people named Williams in the phone book. He couldn't call up each and every one and ask if someone named Tori lived there. Surely Mo would understand that. What if there was another Tori Williams? What if he asked the wrong Tori Williams out on a date?

2. C   Friday morning David put on what he thought were his best and luckiest clothes. He needed all the luck he could get. Not only was he going to ask Tori for her phone number, but also he had to explain to Mo why he hadn't called Tori last night.

Not to mention the fact that the curse was back.

3. B   "By the way," David said, "the curse is back. Of course you don't care about that." "What happened?" asked Larry. He told them about the apple juice pouring onto Elizabeth's face. They both giggled at the word nipple.

4. A   "That's a pretty shirt," she said. "Thanks. It's my lucky shirt." "It's nice. You look like a Greek poet."

5. B   He sat down on the edge of the couch and stared at them. Some of the masks were very odd; faces with three eyes or faces that were half black and half white. There was one that looked like it was part lion and part human, although it was impossible to tell where the lion stopped and the human started. But the eeriest ones looked like real faces.

6. C   Both of Roger's parents probably worked, so there was probably no one home right now. The cane was probably just stuck inside Roger's closet.

7. A   Glen raised his fists. "You want to fight?" he asked. "I'll fight you. I could beat you up just like I beat up Ricky." David stopped. He didn't know what to do. He couldn't very well fight a little kid. "What are you doing home from school?" he demanded.

chapters 29 to 32

1. D   "Anyway, I never lived in Australia," Larry admitted. "I made that up." David felt a sinking feeling in his stomach. Larry had been his one hope. "What about Japan?" he asked. "I never lived outside the U.S. Hey, but don't tell Mo, okay? She thinks I'm a man of the world."

2. C   "You asked me for my phone number," she said. "I closed my eyes as I tried to remember it. I can remember things better when my eyes are closed. When I opened my eyes, you were gone."

3. B   "The lemonade!" exclaimed Tori. "Huh?" "It probably wasn't really lemonade. It was face juice!"

4. D   "She said she'd remove the curse if you returned the cane?" For the first time, Tori seemed genuinely surprised.

5. C   "I don't want honey," he said. He took another sip of tea. "It's good." He smiled at Tori. David watched, amazed. Ricky obviously didn't think Tori was a stooge.

6. B   "I'm going too," she declared. "Me too!" exclaimed Ricky. David looked at his brother. "I don't—" "Glen'll be there," said Ricky. "I want another shot at Glen Delbrook!

7. D   Tori walked up behind them and slipped her arm through David's. "Shall we

take our leave, Mr. Ballinger?" she asked. She was holding the snakehead cane . . . .

1. C   "If you want the curse to be removed," she said, "you better drink." "What about her?" he asked. "Only one thing can save her now," said Mrs. Bayfield. "What?" "First you have to drink." He drank the liquid. It was sweet, but at the same time very sour. "Ahhhhh …" said Mrs. Bayfield as if she had been the one who drank it. "I feel a lot better. We are both now rid of the horrible curse." "You?" asked Mo. "The curse was just as painful for me as it was for Mr. Ballinger," she said. "Maybe even worse for me." "What about Tori?" asked David. He looked at her, rigid like a statue, her face in front of her face. "Kiss her," said Mrs. Bayfield.

2. B   "Why do you keep calling me Mr. Ballinger?" he asked. "That's your name." "Except you call her Tori," he pointed out. "You two know each other. You call me Mr. Ballinger because that's what she always used to call me!"

3. C   "But you did know my name," said David. "And my phone number. I saw it written on a pad of paper." "I wrote that," said Tori. "I called you from here. You probably don't remember. I heard you answer the phone and then I got scared and hung up. I just wanted to find out … I mean, you had been so nice to me and then you suddenly just started ignoring me. I just wanted to find out why. I thought maybe it was something I said, or maybe Maureen was your girlfriend and she didn't want you talking to me."

4. D   "I assure you, David," said Mrs. Bayfield. "If I'd known you'd come back with your face so badly bruised, I would never have asked you to bring me my cane. I'm very sorry about that.

5. B   "If you are cursed, Mr. Ballinger—David," said Mrs. Bayfield, "it is only because you are a sensitive, caring human being."

6. A   "Did you see what David gave me?" asked Tori. "He made it in shop class." "His apple-cheese board!" exclaimed Mo. "It's not an apple-cheese board," said Tori, somewhat offended. "It's a heart."

7. D   Everyone stopped talking. They were on a field trip. It was March 15, 2139. There was no school tomorrow because it was David Ballinger's birthday. … Everyone in his class had had to memorize a famous speech. Willy had chosen Ballinger's Moscow Address.